THE
FOLKLORE
SUPERSTITIONS
and LEGENDS

of BIRMINGHAM
and The
West Midlands

by RICHARD S. BROWN

Westwood Press Publications

44 BOLDMERE ROAD, SUTTON COLDFIELD
WEST MIDLANDS B73 5TD
TELEPHONE: 021-354 5913

The Author — Richard S. Brown

HE WAS BORN IN PEMBROKE, Dyfed in 1935. He was educated at Pembroke Dock Grammar School, St Peter's College Saltley and West Midlands College of Higher Education where he attained a Bachelor of Education (Hons) Degree.

His National Service was in the Royal Air Force where he served at R.A.F. Lichfield and R.A.F. Steamer Point, Aden. He qualified for the teaching profession in 1959 and has been a resident of Sutton Coldfield and taught in Birmingham schools ever since. In 1971 he was appointed Headteacher of Alston Junior School and in 1979 to the headship of Springfield Middle School, his present position.

Richard is married with two daughters. His interests in addition to local history, include natural history, rugby, cricket, snooker, walking, gardening and bee keeping. He began freelance writing in 1985 and he has had articles, poems and stories published in sixteen different national and international magazines.

Dedication
To Ann, Catherine and Rachel.

© Copyright Westwood Press

First Edition Autumn 1992

Printed & Published by The Westwood Press, 44 Boldmere Road Sutton Coldfield, West Midlands. Produced by Offset Litho.

Contents

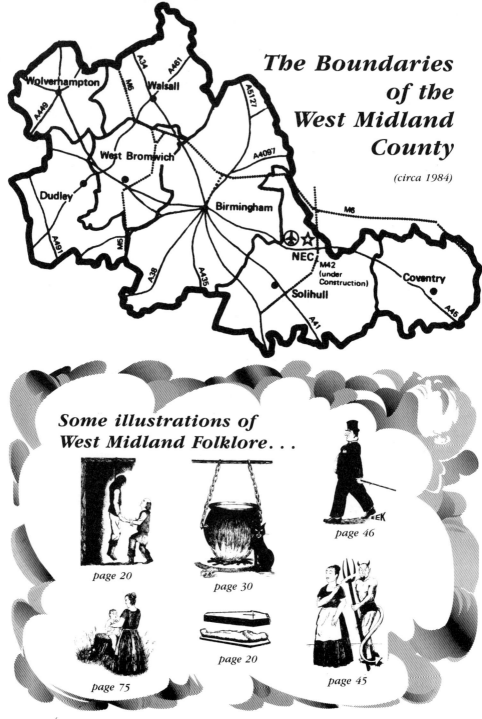

The Boundaries of the West Midland County

(circa 1984)

Wolverhampton
A34
A461
M6
Walsall
A449
A5127
West Bromwich
A4097
Dudley
Birmingham
M6
A491
M5
A38
A435
NEC
M42 (under Construction)
Coventry
A45
Solihull
A41
EEK

Some illustrations of West Midland Folklore...

page 20

page 30

page 46

page 75

page 20

page 45

Introduction

THIS IS THE first book which brings together the folklore, customs, superstitions and legends of Birmingham and the West Midland County. It includes the folklore of the countryside, dating from the Middle Ages, and the customs, beliefs and superstitions of industrial Birmingham, The Black Country, Wolverhampton and Coventry.

The first three chapters deal with birth, marriage and death. Many beliefs and ceremonies concerning these important events have been forgotten or discarded but many are still practised especially those which surround the wedding ceremony.

From the moment of birth a person's whole future could be influenced by the omens, superstitions and beliefs which surrounded his daily life and fear of the powers of witchcraft, goblins and ghosts was ever present. Chapters Five, Six and Seven list some of these influences and some of the ways employed to combat them with charms and cures.

The daily toil at home, and at the workplace, had its own folklore, beliefs and customs as did the sports and pastimes which amused the people in the few hours of leisure permitted after the day's work. Chapters Four and Eight are devoted to these two aspects of every day life in what is now, the West Midland County.

Chapter Nine is comprised of a collection of well known and lesser known stories and ballads from this story-rich county on the edge of Shakespeare land.

The final chapter is a calender of customs associated with the Church and with local ancient rite and custom.

A great deal of folklore was outlawed by the Puritans in the seventeenth century and much was lost or forgotten in the nineteenth century. The Industrial Revolution with mechanisation and changes in work patterns destroyed a great deal of what remained but folklore is now enjoying a revival.

Conservation has become a social and political hot potato. There is a growing demand for natural products, alternative medicine and faith cures. History has become big business, but not just that which highlights the strutting of noblemen but also that of the common people which are at the grass roots of all history.

This book attempts to highlight the hopes and fears of our ancestors in a pre-scientific age, to make us aware of our roots - that the past is part of us.

Richard S. Brown

Foreword

THE WEST MIDLANDS COUNTY came into being in 1974, the largest of the new metropolitan counties set up under the reorganisation of local government. It is the most populous local authority outside of London and spreads across the heartland of England from Wolverhampton in the west to Coventry in the east with Britain's second city, Birmingham set firmly at its centre.

Although the metropolitan authority was abolished in 1986, the new county boundary still encompasses most of those areas which were, prior to 1974, North Warwickshire, South Staffordshire and Greater Birmingham.

The folklore of Warwickshire has been well documented by writers such as J. A. Langford (1875), George Morley (1900), J. Harvey Bloom in his *Folklore, Old Customs and Superstitions of Shakespeare Land* (1929) and most recent Roy Palmer in *The Folklore of Warwickshire* (1976).

Numerous writers have researched and published works on the folklore of Staffordshire. G. T. Lawley was the main collector of material followed by F. W. Hackwood with his *Staffordshire Customs, Superstitions and Folklore* 1924 and John Raven with *The Folklore of Staffordshire* in (1978).

However very little has been written about the folklore of what is now Greater Birmingham, though Roy Palmer, acknowledging this omission collected and included a quantity of material in his excellent book.

This is the first to bring together the folklore, customs, superstitions and legends of Greater Birmingham and the rest of the West Midland County. It contains some well documented folklore but also a quantity of previously unpublished material and more than 90 illustrations.

Acknowledgements

I wish to express my thanks to all who have helped me, directly or indirectly in writing and illustrating this book.

In particular I wish to thank Mr Christopher Weller a student of the Graphics and Printing Department of Matthew Boulton Technical College whose fine illustrations help 'bring the script to life'. Grateful thanks also to Ros Calloway, his tutor who helped us both.

I pay tribute to the many librarians who by their patience and professionalism made my research a little less arduous.

I am most grateful to Ann and to Catherine and Rachael who have encouraged my enthusism for writing.

CHAPTER I

Birth and Early Childhood

THE PRESENT PRACTICE of babies being delivered in hospital is a very recent development, indeed prior to the middle of this century most babies were born at home. The growth of maternity hospitals and pre-natal care has almost completely erased the ancient and widespread belief that a child's whole life and character could be influenced by the many potentially evil powers which surrounded birth.

Eighteenth and nineteenth century parents-to-be dare not ignore such beliefs and every precaution was taken well before the actual birth.

EVIL INFLUENCES

Evil influences before birth were countered by the mother-to-be avoiding any contact with persons who were considered to have the Evil Eye.

This would include those unfortunate people who had a squint, whose eyes were of different colours, set too close together or over deep in the head.

For the pregnant woman to be 'overlooked' by such a person was considered to be very unlucky, even though the afflicted person may have no leanings to evil, and charms in the form of silver coins or objects were carried by the woman at all times.

The time of birth was so important that many baptismal records indicated not only the date and day of the week but also the exact hour and the state of the moon. The astrological belief that the sun, moon and planets have an influence on people's lives is still wide spread and many of us who are unbelievers cannot resist reading our 'stars' in the newspapers.

The earlier the birth was in the day the more fortunate was the child; it had a better chance of reaching old age. A child born at midnight or between midnight and one o'clock was unable to be bewitched. This was also true of the Sunday or Christmas Day child which was everywhere considered to become lucky, strong and clever.

THE UNLUCKIEST DAY OF THE YEAR

To be born on Childermas Day (28th December) was very unlucky. This is the day when it is believed that Herod gave the orders to kill the boy babies and is considered the unluckiest day of the year.

The well known rhyme which begins, 'Monday's child is fair of face', has many versions. The Warwickshire version is:

'Monday's child is fair of face,
Tuesday's child is full of grace,
Wednesday's child if full of woe,
Thursday's child is inclined to
thieving,
Friday's child is free and giving,
Saturday's child works hard for a
living,
But the child that is born on the
Sabbath Day,
Is blithe and bonny, good and
gay'.

Defective children were believed to be changelings or fairy children which had been swopped by the fairy mothers for the human child. Every effort was made to prevent this by filling the delivery room with friends and relatives who kept watch as they assisted.

Throughout the West Midland County it was considered very lucky for a child to be born with a caul, the inner part of the amniotic sac, covering its face or head. It is believed that the child would never drown and that anyone who owned such a membrane would never drown. The dried masks were usually kept within the family but were sometimes sold and often fetched a good sum of money.

In 1813 *The Times* published an advertisement for a caul with the asking price 12 guineas, a very substantial sum.

They were much sought after by sailors, fishermen and others whose daily work brought them into contact with sea, lake or river.

It was common to hand down the masks from one generation to another. The will of Sir John Offley of Madeley, Staffordshire in 1658 describes a piece of gold enamelled jewellery which contained Sir John's own birth mask. This he bequeathed to his daughter and to her son and heirs.

It was also believed in Birmingham, that carrying a dried caul prevented rheumatism.

HAIRCUTS BANNED IN FIRST YEAR

Babies were never weighed at birth or it was believed that they would die within the year and it was considered unlucky to cut a baby's hair or nails before it was twelve months old. Should the child's nails grow too long within the year they were bitten short.

The child's first food was a mixture of butter, sugar and honey which was thought to give sweetness to its tongue.

To make sure that the child would prosper it was the custom to take the child upstairs before going down. Specially prepared structures of furniture and even step ladders, were arranged so that the infant could be physically carried 'upstairs'.

THE PERIL OF EVIL SPIRITS

The new born baby was in constant peril from the evil spirits until it was christened. The best protection was to get the ceremony completed as soon as possible after the birth especially as it was believed that the child would not thrive until christened. If the ceremony had to be delayed it was given protection by charms such as salt, iron or garlic which were placed in the cradle and the chosen name was kept a secret so that witches or fairies could not use it in a spell.

Cats were kept well away from new born children as it was believed that they sucked the life breath out of infants.

It was a bad sign if the baby sneezed during the service but a good sign if it cried. Crying was a sign that the devil was being driven out. Salt was placed in the child's mouth as the 'salt of wisdom' which would give it God's grace for the rest of its life.

God Parents were called Gossips; there were never more than three and parents were not allowed to be God Parents until 1865.

If a sickly child was born and it was considered likely to die the baptism was performed in the home by the midwife. This was known as 'half christened or half baptised'.

If the child survived it was christened in the usual way. If it died, as it was not yet a christian, it was buried in unconsecrated ground on the north side of the church with still-born children and suicides.

THE MOTHER'S CAUDLE

After the delivery it was usual for the mother to remain in the bedroom and she was given a special nourishing mixture of old ale, oatmeal, sugar and spices. This was known as 'caudle' and was collected by the father from the squire's wife whose duty it was to privide it. If no ale was available water drawn from special wells known as 'caudle wells' was substituted.

"CHURCHING" AFTER CHILDBIRTH

After childbirth it was considered very unlucky for a woman to leave her house for any purpose before being 'churched'. To visit another home before the ceremony would bring bad luck on that household. This belief was still held in some parts of the country up to forty years ago.

The christian service of Churching is to give thanks for a safe delivery but, in some christian and biblical times, a woman was considered unclean and was dangerous to herself and others before the cleansing service. It was also believed that she was vulnerable to attacks from such evil forces as witches and fairies.

CHARMS AGAINST SICKNESS AND EVIL

The rate of infant mortality was high and parents relied upon charms to protect the newborn child against sickness and evil influences.

Loops of Wild Clematis were placed around the child to prevent convulsions and pieces of Woody Nightshade, a magical plant used against witches as well as by them, was used for the same purpose.

Whooping Cough or Chin Cough, before the days of vaccination, was a dreaded sickness which killed many babies. Charms against catching the illness and cures for it were widespread.

One of the most common local remedies was to pass the child under and over a natural bridge. Two of the most frequent 'bridges' were a tip rooted bramble and a donkey's belly. Most donkeys have a 'cross' of darker hair on their shoulders in remembrance,

so it is thought, of the fact that Jesus chose it for his last triumphant ride. Hairs plucked from this cross were believed to cure whooping cough, fits, convulsions and prevented toothache and teething troubles. They were chopped finely and administered to the patient in bread and butter.

Cooked mice were fed to children suffering from coughs, colds, fits, whooping cough, sore throats, and infectious fevers. Belief in the curative properties of fried, roasted or baked mice was very common until fairly recent times. Such a cure was prescribed by several correspondents to Tricia Ray, a Sutton Coldfield schoolgirl, who in 1980 became an entry in *The Guinness Book of Records* for non stop sneezing.

TRANSFER OF ILLNESS TO ANIMALS

The magical transfer of illness from patient to animals and plants was believed possible and widely practised in the Midlands. Local people believed that measles, whooping cough, scarlet fever and thrush could be cured by feeding some hairs of a patient to a dog or a donkey. Allowing a piebald horse or a sheep to breathe the sick child's breath was another cure.

Snails were also used as scape goats. The patient ate part of a piece of bread and butter and left the remains outside for the snails to eat.

Thrush or White Mouth was treated by holding the head of a live frog in the infant's mouth so that the ailment was transferred to the creature in the child's breath and spittle.

CURING THE RICKETS

A charm to cure rickets or rupture involved the splitting of a maiden ash sapling. The naked child was then passed nine times through the cleft. It was usual for the father to pass the child to another man and for there to be nine people present. It was vitally important that the tree should recover after the ceremony and the cleft was bound and nailed carefully so that it would heal. The young tree was henceforth protected from damage and destruction as it was believed that the life of the patient depended on the life of the tree.

One such tree is recorded (1804) to have stood in Shirley Heath on the side of the road leading from Hockley to Birmingham.

BIRTHMARKS

Birth marks are often thought to be caused by the pregnant woman seeing or touching something, the shape of the birthmark representing its cause. It was especially unlucky for a mother-to-be to see a hare as it was believed that this animal was often a witch transformed. Should this occur locally the woman would make three rents in her shift thus preventing her child being born with a hare lip.

A common cure for birth mark blemishes was for the mother to lick the disfigurement first thing in the morn-

ing, before she had eaten. This was done as soon as possible after the birth and continued for up to thirty days or until it disappeared. This was recorded as late as the 1950's in this part of the Midlands.

The Font
Aston Parish Church

CHAPTER II

With This Ring

IT WAS RARE FOR GIRLS to go to school. They were expected to help in the home and to learn to cook, sew, clean and look after their brothers and sisters. It is little wonder that they looked forward in a romantic way to a husband of their own, a knight in shining armour to take them away from the daily drudge. Well before marriageable age they amused themselves with games and charms intended to foretell the name of their future husband.

LUCKY CHARMS

Several charms involved the use of magical plants. Ash leaves were thought

to be lucky and an 'even ash', a leaf with an equal number of divisions on each side, especially lucky. If the finder held it and said,

> 'Even ash, I pluck thee off the
> tree,
> The first young man that I
> do meet,
> My lover he shall be',

her wish would come true. She would then put in in her left shoe hidden under her foot and if she slept with it under her pillow, her future husband would appear to her in a dream. A four leafed clover was used in the same way.

An ivy leaf was used in a similar way with the rhyme being:

> 'Ivy, Ivy, I love you,
> In my bosom I put you,
> The first young man who speaks
> to me,
> My future husband he shall be.

A custom common in the Midlands, especially in the Wednesbury area was for a girl to peel an apple, making sure that the peel remained unbroken. She would then stand in an open space and throw the peel over her left shoulder. The paring was then examined to see if it resembled a letter of the alphabet. The letter so found, would be the initial of her future husband.

MAKING A DUMB CAKE

Making a Dumb Cake was a well known charm to produce a vision of a future husband. There were several versions but the Midland version involved three girls. They would together prepare and bake a cake of flour, water, eggs and salt. Once cooked the cake was divided equally and eaten at midnight, then the three girls walked backwards to bed but first they removed every fastening from their dresses. If the

charm has been correctly performed visions of their future husbands would appear and chase them, snatching at their clothes. Once in bed the phantoms disappeared. The whole proceeding had to be done in silence, hence the name Dumb Cake, but it seems unlikely that many such charms were ever conducted without giggles and squeals from the young participants.

The most important dates to enact these ceremonies were St. Mark's Eve (24th April) St. Agnes Eve (20th January) and St. Thomas Eve (21st December).

ENSURING A SUCCESSFUL MARRIAGE

Once a couple were betrothed and the wedding day set every precaution had to be taken to ensure that the marriage would be a success. It was believed to be most unlucky for an engaged couple to hear their banns read in church. This bad luck would manifest itself in an afflication in their future children; they would be born deaf or blind.

Bethrothal was considered almost as binding as the marriage. To cancel a wedding after the final reading was frowned upon both by the community and the church. In some dioceses the couple could be fined by the vicar.

Setting the date was important as certain days, months and holy days were considered unlucky for marriages. Lent, Advent and Easter were all prohibited by the church. The month of May was not though it was considered to be very unlucky and is not popular today.

'Marry in May and rue the day' or 'Marry in May, you'll soon decay' were common, widespread, wise warnings.

The day of the week was important too. The first three days of the week were lucky but Thursday, Friday and Saturday were best avoided. In some parts of this county a couple who were married on a Wednesday were thought to be destined for poverty.

THE RULES FOR THE WEDDING DRESS

The choice and the wearing of the wedding dress was, and still is, governed by strict rules and beliefs.

It was considered unlucky for the bride to make her own dress or to put on her full bridal outfit too soon. She must on no account see herself in the mirror until leaving for church and even then it was thought wise to leave off something small such as gloves or veil.

The colour of the dress was important. White, blue, silver, pink and gold were considered lucky. Blue has always been popular and lucky and something blue, together with something 'borrowed' and 'something old' were included in the final bridal array.

SIGNIFICANCE OF THE WEDDING RING

The wedding ring was deeply significant. Once put on by the husband in church it was considered unlucky to remove it. If it came off by accident or had to be removed then it must be replaced by the husband.

Never-the-less, in the nineteenth century when times were hard, it was not

A typical Wedding Group

uncommon for a woman to borrow a ring or use a curtain ring or even on occasions, the ring of the church key. To drop the ring, or worse still lose it was most unfortunate as it was a guard against child sickness.

An old, borrowed bridal veil was considered to be luckier than a new one especially if it belonged to a woman who was happily married. It was never to be put on before the dress and should be the last item donned before leaving for the church.

ON THE WAY TO THE CHURCH

The journey to the church was strewn with unlucky pitfalls. To guard against bad luck the bride would leave the house, right foot first over the threshold. It was lucky for the sun to shine on her or for her to see a rainbow.

If she or any of the wedding party, saw a chimney sweep in full working attire or a black cat, on the way to the

14

ceremony it was a good sign. Grey horses were lucky too and bridal carriages were always drawn by greys.

The worst thing to encounter was a funeral. even to see one in the distance was considered ill luck.

The present custom of the bride and groom not seeing each other before the wedding was common though not universal. Walking weddings were popular in rural areas with the procession led by the bride and the best man followed by the groom and bridesmaids. On the return journey the newly weds led the procession.

It was quite common in working class areas for neither sets of parents-in-law to be present at the church.

WEDDING CAKE

Wedding cake is a very ancient part of the marriage feast. Traditionally it was made of the finest ingredients with the mixture being as rich as possible to indicate abundance.

After the ceremony the bride, assisted by the groom, would cut or break the cake and distribute it to all present to eat. The bride would retain a piece to guard against husband infidelity and to eat at the christening of the first child. The bridesmaids sometimes kept a piece of cake and slept with it under their pillows hoping that its powers may induce visions of their future husbands. The cake would be particularly potent as a charm if passed nine times through a wedding ring before placing under a pillow.

Rice or grains of wheat would be thrown at the couple to indicate fertility and fruitfulness.

CELEBRATIONS AFTER THE CEREMONY

Once the ceremony was complete the day was marked in various ways. Sometimes a two-handed loving cup would be passed around the village, and often a 'bride' cup was circulated in the church. In the area of the West Midlands which was South Staffordshire most weddings were followed by a gathering together of relatives, friends and local villagers who took part in various types of games. A popular game was football which was played in large

numbers in the streets and lanes. The ball was provided by the bridegroom and was known as the 'bride' ball.

The bride would use a handful of cinders from her mother's house to kindle her first fire in her new home and once kindled it was hoped that it would never go out.

In some parts of the county it was one of the duties of the bridesmaids to undress the bride on her wedding night and lay her on the bed. The girl who drew the first pin was thought to be lucky for she would be the next to marry. She could not keep it as all the pins had to be thrown away otherwise the charm would not work or the present marriage would not prosper.

ROUGH MUSIC FOR ADULTERY!

Despite these many precautions domestic bliss was not always achieved. Those who were guilty of breaking the local code of morals were often subjected to 'Rough Music' or 'Lewbelling' as it was known locally. Acts of adultery, wife or husband beating, total domination by either husband or wife, incest, marriage to a woman of ill morals or any sexual crime were, from early times, considered to bring crop failure and disaster upon the whole community.

Rough music meant exactly that. The punishment was enacted by the men and boys of the parish who in procession and at the dead of night beat upon cooking utensils, blew whistles and horns and generally made as much noise as possible.

Sometimes life-like models of the offenders were carried on a pole or in a small cart and burnt outside the miscreant's door, outside the church or in some nearby open space.

Straw or chaff was often laid at the door of persistent offenders or that of villagers whose conduct was causing concern.

'The term 'Lewbelling' is believed to come from 'lewd' and 'belling' (roaring or bellowing)' (*The Illustrated London News* 1909)

THE PRACTICE OF WIFE SELLING

When a marriage had totally broken down an unofficial form of divorce or 'Wife Selling' was practised. Numerous wife sales are recorded in eighteenth and nineteenth century press reports.

The sale of a wife had to be done publicly with the wife's consent and according to traditional procedure. The woman had to be led by a halter to the place of the sale and couldn't be sold for less than one shilling. Both parties were, afterwards, allowed to re-marry.

The Annual Record 1773 records the sale, by Samuel Whitehouse of Willenhall of his wife, Mary Whitehouse to Thomas Griffiths of Birmingham for one guinea.

The Wolverhampton Chronicle, November 1837, describes the sale of the wife of George Hutchinson, named Elizabeth, to Thomas Snape of Burntwood. The sale took place at Walsall Market and the agreed price was two shillings and sixpence. Hutchinson was said to be glad to get rid of 'his frail rib' as she had been living with Snape for three years.

Wife selling has never been legal in Britain but the practice was common, particularly in the lower classes, until 1857 when divorce became legal for the first time. Though available divorce was expensive and wife selling continued to be practised.

There are no local records of wives selling husbands.

———— •●• ————

CHAPTER III

Dust to Dust

'MAN THAT IS BORN of woman has but a short time to live . . . in the midst of life we are in death'. These simple lines from The Burial Service underline the one sure thing about life, the inevitability of death, and death rites and ceremonies are important aspects of Midland folk lore.

heard with trepidation and dreams of insects or lost teeth were omens of ill luck.

The tap of a Death Watch Beetle was an ominous sound and, rather surpris-

OMENS OF DEATH

Death warnings or omens were often associated with animals and plants. The raven, a bird of ill omen, seen flying over a particular house was a death warning to the occupants and if a bird, especially a white bird, flew against a window it was a sign that the angel of death was near at hand.

At night the howling of a dog, the screech of an owl or a cock crow were

ingly, the perching of a robin on a house on Christmas Day forbade ill luck and death.

Fruit trees blooming or bearing fruit out of season, being rare and unnatural occurrences, spelt misfortune and the blossoms of flowering shrubs, especially hawthorn blossoms, were never taken into the house.

The transplanting of parsley, which is usually sown in situ and thinned, was considered such a misdeed as to bring death to the family of the foolish gardener.

LOCAL SUBSTITUTE FOR MAGICAL MANDRAKE

White Briony, a common intrusive climbing plant of the West Midlands, was treated with the same respect as the magical Mandrake which is not indigenous. Both plants have huge fleshy tuberous roots. To cut through one even by accident, was a portent of death and they were unearthed with great care and respect.

Spades, shovels or other excavating tools were never carried into the house at the end of the day. To do so, especially if carried on the shoulder, was putting one's kinsfolk in jeopardy. Brooms were never bought in May because:

'If you buy a broom in May,
You're sure to sweep a corpse
away'.

Imperfections in the tallow of a candle would sometimes cause the flame to splutter resulting in strange curled or winding formations in the melted fat. These were known locally as 'winding sheets' or palls and were undeniable warnings.

Cinders spitting out of the hearth, a marble rolling downstairs, a picture or a flitch of bacon falling off a hook, a mouse on the bed or a clock striking thirteen were all happenings of ill omen.

Square or diamond shaped creases discovered whilst unfolding newly laundered table linen were known as 'coffins' and were obvious warnings.

HELPING A PATIENT TO DIE EASILY

Once death was accepted as inevitable it was not uncommon for the relatives to 'help' the patient to die easily. A widespread belief was that to lie on a pillow or mattress which contained game bird or pigeon feathers would hinder death and so cause the dying person unnecessary suffering. These were avoided or removed.

Shock treatment which involved placing the dying person onto the cold bare floor or the practice of 'drawing the pillow' were other methods of death easing. In the latter case the pillows on which the sick person lay were whipped away without warning with the resultant whip of the head and neck resulting in death.

THE RITUALS AFTER DEATH

After death there were several important duties and rituals to perform. Coins were placed on the eyes so that they remained closed and all locks and bolts in the house were unfastened so that the spirit could be released. A plate of salt was placed on the chest to keep away evil spirits and mirrors were covered or turned to the wall. All furniture which had been used by the deceased was covered with white cloths and all perishable foods were removed from the household.

Pet dogs, cats and birds were ejected as it was believed that they would hinder the spirit but the household stocks of honey bees were told of their master's death otherwise they would not thrive.

Local inhabitants who could afford to, sometimes kept a linen sheet edged with lace to cover the corpse. These were handed down from generation to generation.

GOING OUT FEET FIRST

The corpse remained in a darkened room, in the house until the funeral. It was then carried through the front door of the house, always feet first. The mourners followed with the closest and eldest first and then two abreast in order of age. All wore black, or some black, as a sign of respect. It was considered bad luck to wear black before the funeral. The front door was left open until the funeral returned.

Superstitions concerning the procession and burial were legion. If the sun shone on a mourner he could very well be the next one to go; if it rained at a funeral it meant that the deceased was 'happy' and no doubt the mourners relieved.

A rhyme common throughout Britain says:

'Happy is the bride that the sun shines on
Happy is the corpse that the rain falls on'.

It was unlucky to meet a funeral and desperately unlucky for newly weds to catch even a fleeting glimpse of a funeral. Funeral horses were black or grey. Should these animals become restless or stubborn or toss their heads and neigh in the direction of a house there would be a funeral there within the year.

It was considered very bad luck for the dear departed's soul to be the first buried in a new cemetery or to be the last buried in a full cemetery. Sometimes a dog or other domestic animal was secretly buried there to avoid this ill luck.

Gravestones — Holy Trinity Church, Sutton Coldfield

RE-USEABLE COFFINS WERE COMMONPLACE

Parish coffins with detachable bottoms were common place and saved considerable expense. The coffin was lowered into the grave and the four sides and roof were detached leaving the corpse covered with a pall, and the floor of the coffin to be interred.

The north side of the churchyard was rarely used except for the unbaptised and suicides.

Headstones were not common but body stones which cover the length of the grave, and often bore the sign of the cross, were used as long ago as the fifteenth century. Graves were sited east/west with the feet to the west.

————— ••• —————

THE HANGMANS TOUCH AS A CURE ALL

It was believed that the touch of a man's hand who had been hanged or who had committed suicide could cure such ailments as goitre, cancer. sores and even barrenness. Hangmen were

sometimes bribed to allow the infected part of a sufferer to be touched by the death hand.

Sin-Eating was quite common. A poor individual who needed food and money would sometimes be engaged by the relatives of the deceased to take on the sins of the dead man by sin-eating. Bread and beer were passed over the coffin to this poor unfortunate who, together with these victuals, imbibed the remaining sins.

A common belief was that the sound of church bells would drive away demons because bell music came from holy things. The tolling of a single bell followed by three clear strokes indicated the funeral of a child. Six strokes were traditional for a woman and nine for a man.

It was traditional, and still is, to decorate with flowers the graves of loved ones on their birth date and the anniversary of their death. The increase in the number of cremations is gradually erasing this ancient custom.

CHAPTER IV

Daily Toil

THE DAILY TOIL AT home and at workplace had its own folklore; beliefs and customs which were often associated with the season or month of the year.

PLOUGH MONDAY

Christmas was celebrated for the full twelve days ending on Twelfth Night which was a final chance to make merry before the arduous work of ploughing began on the first Monday following. This was known as Plough Monday. On that day it was customary for ploughmen and boys to drag a plough bedecked with ribbons through the village, accompanied by whatever music was available, and making a collection at each house.

Traditional fare for the day was boiled beef and carrots with plum pudding to follow.

The plough used to till the soil was drawn by four pairs of oxen which were preferred to horses as they needed less care and attention at the day's end. The oxen were 'broken' by yoking them to a heavy log and turning them out to pasture. When sufficiently tired they were introduced to harness. Horses were used too. They were much prized and great care was taken when making a purchase at one or other of the numerous horse fairs.

AN EARLY START TO SOWING

Beans were an important crop and being quite hardy, were sown as soon as the soil was friable enough to walk on and to take a dibber. This was usually about mid-February and in some places started on St. Valentine's Day. The beans were sown four at a time to cater for loss by bird and small animal predation.

Peas and corn were broadcast. The seed, carried in a leather hopper by the sower was scattered on either side as he strode the field with measured tread. 'The hyer and farther that ye caste your corne the better shall it spread'. For this cold, tiring day's work they would get one shilling.

Young children were employed to protect the seed from the voracious crows and pigeons. Shaking rattles and

clappers these cold, lonely children spent the total daylight hours in the fields for four pence per day.

A song from the fields where Handsworth now stands is recorded in the *Birmingham Weekly Post* 1881 (Oct-Nov).

> '*Cooo-oo!*
> *I've got a pair of clappers*
> *And I'll knock 'e down back'ards*
> *I've got a great stone,*
> *And I'll knock your backbone'.*

POSY TO START THE HAYMAKING

By the mid-summer the crops were well established and it was time to mow the meadows to make hay. On the first day of hay making each man received a posy for his wife, or sweetheart, which was pinned to her smock. They were

expected to help their husbands and were paid six pence a day.

The farmer provided a barrel of beer to refresh the labourers and the gamekeeper supplied a further barrel to remind the mowers to beware of sitting game birds.

There was usually a short break between the hay and cereal harvest with the latter being the climax of the farming year.

A SACRIFICE TO THE CORN SPIRIT

The reapers were afraid to actually cut the last swathe of corn. It was a widespread custom for the workers to take it in turns to throw their sickles at it so that no-one could be accused of killing the corn spirit. Once cut in this way, a few strands were plaited into a corn dolly. This was kept until the next

year and ceremoniously buried in a furrow on Plough Monday.

A cruel custom, which may be a relic of sacrifice to the corn spirit was often enacted.

A cockerel was tied by one leg, with a length of string, to a stake in an open part of the field. The men then shot or threw sticks and stones at the poor bird hoping to win the bird as a prize for the family pot. The winner achieved this by knocking the bird over and picking it up before it had recovered.

A FEAST FOR THE HARVEST

The last load was brought in with much delight and merriment. The horses were decorated with flowers and ribbons and as many workers as could, rode on the waggon. It was traditional for the driver to be dressed in women's clothes and those who couldn't ride walked behind singing and blowing horns.

The mistress greeted them with cakes and ale and, either that evening or in the next few days, the Harvest Feast took place.

Some of these feasts were elaborate affairs but most took the form of a simple feast in barn or kitchen of boiled beef and carrots and plum pudding washed down with plenty of ale. By the end of the nineteenth century the more lavish celebrations had discontinued.

THE PAYMENT OF TITHES AS 'INCOME' TAX

The paying of tithes of 'tenths' existed well into the nineteenth century.

One in ten of the shucks of corn were collected from the field by the 'parson's men' as a simple income tax.

Gleaning or 'leasing' as it was known locally, was a small perk for the farm workers. The women and children went into the fields and collected any ears of corn which had been missed or dropped. The signal that leasing was to begin was given by the blast of a horn or sometimes the ringing of the church bells.

The small store of grain which accrued was stored in the best bedroom to be used by the household. Wheat was used for baking flour and the barley for malt for the home brewing.

A PANCAKE FOR THE FIRST BORN LAMB

The first born lamb was greeted with much excitement. The shepherd was presented with a pancake and in some areas the 'throwing at cocks' as previously described was practised.

Sheep shearing always took place as the moon grew, usually around the beginning of June. Everyone capable of using a pair of shears took part and then followed a feast of stuffed chine, cider and ale.

Women were expected to help to reap and gather in the crops, feed the pigs, calves and poultry and milk the cows. They also had to wash, sew, cook, care for their husbands and children and keep the house clean and tidy.

THE STAFF OF LIFE

The baking of bread was done weekly. The dough was made in a 'dough kiver' which was an important piece of furniture. Bread is known universally as the 'staff of life' because it has always been the main article of diet for the common man. It also has great religious significance to christians because of its association with the Eucharist. It was considered almost a

*Millstones
from
Sarehole Mill,
Birmingham*

Sarehole Mill — a Water Mill

24

sin to throw it away or to burn it as this act was likely to bring ill luck.

There were many superstitions associated with bread and baking. Most important was the hand kneading to prevent pockets of air which when the bread was baked, formed 'coffins' which were considered to be death omens. Each batch of dough was marked with a cross before putting it into the oven to protect it from the power of the Devil and witches.

Marking was always done with the edge of a knife. Never with the point or cutting edge or with a skewer or fork:

> *'She who pricks the loaf with fork*
> *or knife,*
> *Shall never be happy as maid*
> *or wife'.*

Brewing was done in March and October. The March brew had herbs including stinging nettles and blackcurrant added and was indeed a sort of herb beer. The October brew was a pure malt ale. When the brew was complete it was the custom for neighbours to 'take the first shot' by sampling the new beer by 'dipping' crusts of bread.

The washing was done fortnightly using lye prepared from wood ash in preference to soap. Clothes were never washed on New Year's Day or Good Friday as it would cause a death in the family. Washing was always done at the beginning of the week so that the garments would be well dried and ironed for Sunday. Saturday washing was an indication of a bad housewife:

> *'Wash on a Friday, wash in need*
> *Wash on a Saturday, a slut*
> *indeed.'*

Diamond shaped creases or 'coffins' which sometimes occur in folded table or bed linen were death omens.

WAGES WERE GRADED FOR SKILLS

Skilled men earned roughly twice as much as labourers. In the building trade the highest paid were master masons and joiners followed by plasters and carpenters.

The wood trade was important locally and there were shearers, carders and weavers. Blacksmiths and chimney sweeps were important members of the community.

Coventry was known for the quality of its ribbon weaving and especially for the blue dye used there. The saying 'Tried and true like Coventry blue' refers to this and Coventry City Football Team is still known as 'The Sky Blues'.

COLLIERS WERE HIGHLY SUPERSTITIOUS

Coal was mined to the east and west of the West Midland County. Miners like others whose daily work is in a hazardous environment, were very superstitious and they refused to work if the omens were wrong.

Amy Lyons in her *Black Country Sketches* (1901) records that at The Cock Fighter's Arms, Wednesbury there was a painted board fixed to the tap

25

16th Century Barn at Avoncroft Museum

A Black Country Nail Shop

room chimney breast which read as follows:

Ye Colliers Guide to Signs and Warnings

1. To dream of a broken shoe:
2. If you mete a woman at the rising of the sun, turn again from ye pit—a sure sign of death.
3. To dream of fire is a sure sign of danger.
4. To see a bright light in ye mine is a sure sign to flee away.
5. If Gabriel's hounds been aboute, do not work that day.
6. When foule smell be about, ye pit, a sure sign that ye imps be anear.
7. To charm away ghosts and ye Like: take a bible and a key, hold both in ye right hand and say ye Lord's Prayer and they will right speedily get farre away.

To meet a woman on the way to the pit was bad luck especially a cross eyed one. To meet a one legged man or to see a robin perched on a man made object was also bad luck.

Gabriel's Hounds or The Seven Whistlers as they are sometimes known

Time Clock from the Grove Colliery, used for "clocking in"

have been identified in various places as wild geese, curlews, plovers, widgeon and other birds which fly at night calling plaintively as they fly. As it indicates above no man would enter the pit if they 'ben aboute'.

The friendly mine goblins known as Knockers gave warning of danger by making knocking sounds deep in the earth.

Colliers wouldn't work until a dead workmate had been buried and to whistle underground was strictly forbidden.

APPRENTICES HAD TO PAY THEIR 'FOOTINGS'

Apprentices, those learning a new trade or workmen starting at a new workplace had to pay 'footings' or 'foot ale'. This involved buying quantities of ale for their new workmates. If the new hand refused to pay the others would strike or prevent him working until he complied.

Initiation ceremonies of apprentices were also common. These were sometimes dangerous and although practical jokes are still played on young people in their first jobs, they are generally quite harmless.

When an apprenticeship was complete, at his 21st birthday, his master and workmates joined him in a celebration during a prolonged dinner hour and an evening of eating, drinking and dancing.

THE QUAINT FEAST DAY OF 'ST. MONDAY'.

Birmingham men were notorious for the irregularity of their working hours. Many of them took 'St. Monday' as a holiday to indulge their pleasures and sometimes Tuesday too. Those who did not want to lose earnings concentrated the whole weeks work into the remaining days.

A Black Country Chain Shop at Avoncroft Museum

*Part of
the interior of a
Black Country
Small Chain Shop*

CHAPTER V

Witches, Wise Men, Fairies and The Devil

THE LIFE AND WELL being of simple folk was constantly under threat from The Devil and his earthly helpers, witches. The threat of witchcraft was ever present though not all witches were evil.

White witches were friendly and by their 'wort cunning' or knowledge of simple herb cures were able to assist folk with medicines, cures and charms. Grey witches were neither good nor bad but black witches were the enemies of all that was good. They, it was believed, had made a pact with the Devil, signed in their blood, surrendering to him their bodies and souls. His gift to them were familiars in such earthly form as black cats or toads which carried out their evil wishes.

THE PENALTY FOR WITCHCRAFT WAS DEATH

Such was the fear of their power that around two thousand people in Britain were put to death for the practice of witchcraft with many more in Europe. In 1736 a law was made in England which said that witches could no longer be put to death. Despite this the fear of witchcraft persisted well into the nineteenth century and witch covens still exist in Britain. A article in *The Sutton Coldfield Observer,* 27th January 1989, a revelation by an ex-witch, tells of a coven at Streetly.

The witches' calendar was highlighted by eight important dates when it was believed that witches met

together at secret places. These sabats were Candlemas (Feb 1st), The Spring Equinox (March 20th), May Eve (April 30th), The Summer Solstice or Mid-Summers Eve (June 23rd), August Eve (July 31st), the Autumn Equinox (September 20th), Hallowe'en (October 31st) and the Festival of Rebirth (December 20th). The witches would anoint themselves with a special flying ointment made from Deadly Nightshade

A favourite venue for this ceremony, which lasted up to the nineteenth century, was Wryley, near Walsall.

Another Mid-Summer belief was that if girls ran naked around the Roll Right Stones on that evening, they might see a vision of the man they were to marry.

WITCHES COULD CHANGE INTO ANIMAL FORM

Witches, it was believed, could change themselves into animal form. Most feared were black cats, hares,

and Hemlock, given to them by the Devil, and fly to their secret gatherings on their broomsticks.

MIDSUMMER NIGHT RITUALS

In the South Staffordshire area it was believed that on Midsummers Night witches held a sabat or 'Parliament' on the moon at which they would decide the fate of mortal men. It was the local custom for people to decorate their houses with flowers, leaves and herbs to keep away the evil spirits.

Great bonfires were built on the tops of hills and 'sun wheels' which were waggon wheels covered with tar-smeared sacking and string, were constructed. As darkness fell the bonfires, surrounded by all the local people, were lit to resounding dancing and singing. Babies were passed around the flames to protect them from witchcraft and young people leapt and danced around until the fire died. The great sun wheels were ignited and sent careering down the hillsides to symbolise the shortening of daylight. At the end of the ritual the older folk guided the others home by the light of burning brands which also afforded protection from evil spirits.

white rabbits, weasels and even white mice. Hares were especially feared by pregnant women as the mere sight of that creature could deform the child. It would be born with a hare lip, the mark of the Devil.

A pregnant woman who did catch sight of a hare was advised to rent her petticoats three times to counteract the evil influence.

30

Travellers were frightened if they saw a hare at the start of a journey as it could spell disaster. It was only possible to kill a witch in animal form if a silver bullet was used.

Countless stories abound of witches being harmed when transformed into animals. Should some poor old woman, who was suspected of being a witch, develop aches and pains in her legs or arms someone, it would appear, would claim that he had wounded a cat, a hare or a rabbit in the relevant limb.

Such a woman, Sarah Brookes of Knowle was said to sometimes assume the form of a black cat. A cat was wounded in the forepaw when a cruel local lad threw a pitchfork at it. From that day onwards, it is said, poor Sarah had a painful arm which she carried in a sling.

PROTECTION FROM EVIL SPIRITS

Country folk went to great lengths to prevent evil spirits from affecting their work, their animals or their products.

Rowan or Mountain Ash

Shire Horse with Brasses

Milk and butter making were considered especially vulnerable. It was considered unlucky for anyone to enter the dairy whilst the butter was being made but the bad luck could be eradicated if the visitor helped with the work. Witches hate silver and a silver coin was sometimes thrown into the cream. Sometimes a red hot poker was thrust into the mixture which was also considered a guard against witchcraft.

The Rowan or Mountain Ash was often planted as a guard against witches and a sprig of the tree, passed anti-clockwise around a churn, was considered sufficient to do the trick.

Occasionally individuals or mobs, sought revenge on some poor wretched woman suspected of witchcraft, causing her grievous bodily harm and sometimes death.

THE EVIL EYE

The Warwickshire Advertiser, September 1875 records the trial of a local labourer John Hayward, for the murder of eighty year old Ann Tennant from Long Compton. In his defence Hayward claimed that the evil eye of the woman had caused the sickness and death of his farm animals. He was found guilty and ordered to be detained during Her Majesty's Pleasure and he died soon after in Warwick Gaol.

During the trial Hayward begged that she may be weighed against the Church Bible. This was a well known practice for detecting witches. Anyone who outweighed the bible was innocent.

A common belief was that a witche's power could be broken by drawing her blood especially if it was 'above the breath' which involved cutting the witch above the nose or mouth. Shakespeare mentions this brutal charm breaking practice in Henry VI Part 1.

'Blood will I draw from thee,
thou art a witch
And straightway give thy soul
to him who thou serv'st.

THE DUDLEY DEVIL

Local history indicates that it was not the sole prerogative of women to practise witchcraft indeed it seems that there were as many 'cunning men' as 'wise women'.

One such man named Dunn, known locally as The Dudley Devil, was able to do the most extraordinary things. Dunn who died in 1851, claimed to recover stolen articles by the use of charms. His reputation was so great that he drew clients from as far away as London and even Scotland. These clients were not solely from the poorer classes. Many were well to do and Dunn made a very respectable living by his 'magic' powers.

Records indicate that Dunn's success in recovering stolen goods was due to detailed enquiry and observation akin to that of Sherlock Holmes. It seems likely that it was his reputation for detective work and the fear of being apprehended which caused the thieves to replace the stolen articles.

Dunn is buried at Netherton, near Dudley.

Church registers at Wolverhampton record that in 1529 a 'wise man' was consulted about silver plate which had been stolen from a church and that at the latter part of the sixteenth century church wardens at Bilston also consulted a 'wise man' concerning the theft of church property.

MYTHS OF THE FAIRY RINGS

Fairy rings which appear in pasture land are caused by fungal spores radiating in every direction from a central point. In a pre-scientific age people believed that they were places where fairies danced or were the boundaries of underground fairy villages. They believed that if anyone ran nine times clockwise around a fairy ring by the light of the full moon they would hear the fairies laughing. It was bad luck to exceed nine times or to go anti-clockwise or 'widdershins'.

It was considered best to avoid any contact with fairies so it was foolhardy to sit inside a fairy ring especially on May Eve or Hallowe'en. It was dengerous to attempt to destroy a fairy ring, as revenge, in some form of enchantment, would follow.

THE GOOD FAIRIES

Fairies, like witches could be good or bad. The beautiful little people so beloved of children who spend their lives doing nothing but good often feature in local folk lore. Only those with special gifts or possessing special charms ever saw them, but occasionally, when taken unawares, they could be seen singing and dancing in their magic rings.

There were, it was believed, less charming creatures that would steal away a new born child and swop it for one of their own so that the fairy child would have the benefit of human milk and care. The changeling or fairy child was often mal-formed or mentally retarded.

To be kind to fairies by leaving food around the house for them to eat was a wise act. The grateful little people would often repay such kindness by doing household chores.

Friendly fairies known as 'Knockers' were believed to inhabit the local coal mines. They have been described as one and a half feet tall and grotesquely ugly. They dressed in a collier's garb and carried tiny lanterns. They warned of danger by tapping but were also blamed for stealing candles and hiding articles of clothing and tools.

WILL O' THE WISP

The most mischievous of local fairies was Jack O'Lantern or Will O' the Wisp' whose favourite pastime was leading people astray. He sometimes infuriated people by playing tricks on them and on occasions could be sullen and spiteful.

Lob-Lie-By the Fire was a local fairy who could be helpful or downright awkward. He was said to be happy to do house work in exchange for food but if offended would drag the bedclothes off sleepers, put out the fire, cause falls of soot and desert the household.

Fairies chose the site of Knowle Church and of St. Matthews, Walsall. On both occasions the site chosen by the church was not to their liking and the foundation stones were moved repeatedly until the fairy site was accepted.

Robin Goodfellow was known throughout Britain. He was an amusing imp who, though fond of pranks, was never malicious.

LOCAL HOB GOBLINS

A malicious goblin features in *The Legend of The Gilbertstone* (see *Stories and Legends,* Chapter 9) and a flick through street names in the *Birmingham A-Z Street Atlas* indicates that there was a belief in hob goblins e.g. Hob Lane (Sheldon), Hob Moor Road (Yardley) Hobgoblin's Lane (Fillongley). Northfield has Hob Acre, First Hob

A "Knocker"

Knowle Parish Church

Ridge, Far Hob Ridge, Hob Redding and Hob Croft. At Solihull there are Hob's Moat, Hob Moor and Hoberdy's Lantern.

SATAN AND THE DEVIL'S BUSH

Satan, the personification of all that is evil, was said to have been cast out of Heaven on 11th October. He was believed to have fallen into a blackberry bush and has ever afterwards spoilt the berries after that date. Children were told to avoid eating the fruit after 11th October because he had spit or stamped on them or wiped them with his tail.

J. Harvey Bloom 1930 writes,

'All blue flowers are Devil's
flowers and unlucky especially
the Germander Speedwell.
Love in a Mist is also known as
Devil in a bush'.

Nuts have been a symbol of fertility since pagan times and in many countries

St. Michael and the Devil
at Coventry Cathedral

34

a good crop of nuts foretold plenty of births the following year. Should anyone gather nuts on 21st September, which was known as the Devil's Nutting Day, he or she may encounter the evil one himself gathering nuts and stowing them in his grey nutting bag. 'The colour of the Devil's Nutting bag' was a common local saying and indicated anything which was dingy or dirty.

Parsley and potatoes were planted on Good Friday because it was believed that the soil was free from the power of the Devil.

To burn elder wood or to bring it into the house was 'bringing in the Devil' and was likely to cause a death within that household. It was however used in charms against witchcraft and in healing potions.

BIRDS OF THE DEVIL

Birds with pied or black and white feathers were associated with the Devil. Magpies, legend tells us, have black and white feathers because they refused to go into full mourning at the time of the crucifixion.

Sparrows were said to guard the Devil's fire and swallows and swifts were known as Devil Birds.

Yellow Hammers were also associated with the Devil, possibly because of the strange purple scribble marks on their eggs which resemble mysterious writing.

In *Feareful News from Coventry* a pamphlet dated 1642 is recorded the death of Thomas Holte, a Coventry musician who sold himself to the Devil because of financial problems.

George Sacheverell who lived at New Hall, Sutton Coldfield at the end of the eighteenth century was believed to be in league with the Devil. He was known to practise alchemy and recent renovations to the Hall has revealed a room which could have been his secret study.

*The
Three Tuns
Sutton
Coldfield*

*The White Swan
at Harbourne*

CHAPTER VI

Ghosts

GHOST STORIES ABOUND in The West Midland County with haunted buildings ranging from such an historic mansion as Aston Hall to a public telephone box in Erdington.

Colin Smith, a Birmingham ghost hunter, attributes their presence in such numbers to the cruel history of The Civil War.

HAUNTED PUBS AND HOTELS

The White Swan Inn at Harborne is said to be haunted by the ghost of John Wentworth who committed suicide there. Wentworth, who was a man of some standing in the area, had been having an illicit affair with a local girl of somewhat lower status than he. He had arranged to rendez-vous with her in a private room at the inn and had sent a coach to collect her. The unfortunate young woman sustained a fatal accident en route and died in the love nest in her lover's arms. Wentworth, distraught with grief, shot first his dog and then himself.

The White Hart, Walsall is said to be haunted by another suicide, a young woman who died there last century. One hundred and twenty three years ago the mummified arm of a child was found in an attic. It was believed to be linked with witchcraft and possibly with the haunting. This grisly relic is still retained in the Walsall public library.

The cellar of The Three Tuns, Sutton Coldfield is believed to be haunted by the ghost of a drummer boy executed by the Roundheads during the Civil War and another Sutton Coldfield public house, The Gate has a ghost which has been seen dressed in historic clothing, in the ladies toilet.

Strange unexplained happenings at The Queen's Hotel, Wolverhampton were reported in *The Express and Star* in December 1974. Bumps and bangs from the cellar were linked with the spirits of long dead actors from The Queen's Music Hall which used to stand nearby.

Another article in the same newspaper reports a haunting at The Manor House Restaurant, West Bromwich. Strange noises, unexplained singing and reported sightings of an old woman have caused speculation as to the spectres identity but there is no clear evidence and it remains anonymous.

GHOSTLY MONKS

Several local churches are said to be haunted. Fillongley Church is believed to be haunted by monks. Ghosts in monks habits have been seen in the Lady Chapel and residents have felt a strange presence whilst walking the narrow path to the church door.

A headless ghost at St Nicholas Church, Curdworth guards the remains of soldiers killed in The Civil War and a female phantom dressed in a long green gown has also been seen in the churchyard.

THE BODY SNATCHERS

Villains of the past would stop at nothing to line their purses with gold or silver. Body snatchers or 'diggum uppers' as they were known in Birmingham, operated their vile trade long after the Anatomy Act of 1832 which controlled the supply of corpses to medical schools. The Birmingham Medical School, in Edmund Street was a short distance from Warstone Lane Cemetery which it is said, provided rich pickings of newly buried corpses for the 'snatchers'. Since 1946 there have been several sightings of a woman dressed in

St. Nicholas, Curdworth

white crinoline near the cemetery and in the local factories including The Birmingham Mint. This phantom known as 'The White Lady of Warstone' always leaves behind a smell of pear drops. The identity of the lady remains a mystery but there could be a link with the 'diggum uppers' of the nineteenth century.

LAYING A GHOST

In 1881 the Rev. Rooker, vicar of St James Church, Lower Gornal was anxious to exorcise a ghost which haunted the churchyard. He was advised by one of his parishioners, to cut a four inch square turf from the grave of a young man, who it was believed, couldn't rest in his grave. Then the turf was to be placed under the Communion Table where it should stay for four days, thereafter all souls would be laid to perfect rest.

'Wise Men' were sometimes called upon to lay a ghost. The spirit was visited at mid-night and the 'wise man' carrying a bible in his right hand and a key in the other would continuously chant the Lord's Prayer, sometimes backwards.

STATELY HOMES AND CASTLES

Aston Hall, the magnificent house built to completion by Sir Thomas Holte in 1635, has an upper room known as Dick's Garret. This room, thought to be used for servants quarters, is said to be haunted by a suicide who hanged himself there after being rejected by a lover.

———— •••• ————

*Monument to
the Holte Family
in Aston Parish Church*

West Midlands County

MANCHESTER

CANNOCK CHASE

Cannock

Lichfield

Wolverhampton

Walsall

Dudley

Stourbridge

CLENT HILLS

Stratford on Avon Canal

LICKEY HILLS

BRISTOL

Scale: 1 inch to 4 miles

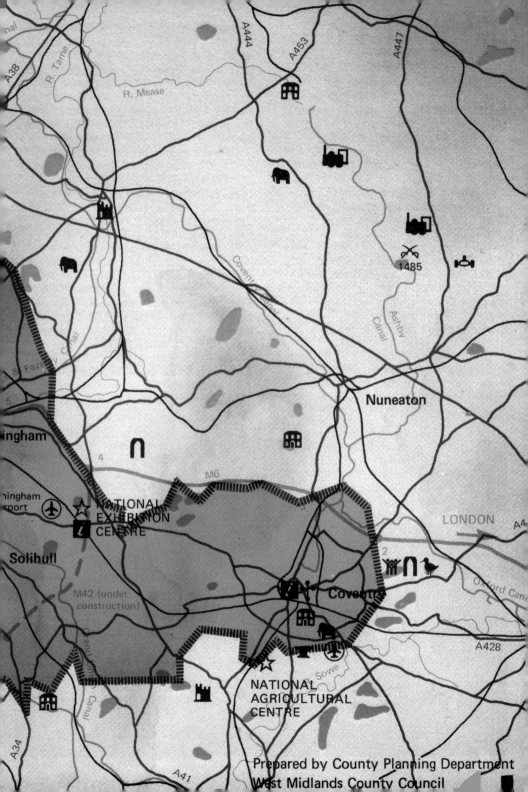

Prepared by County Planning Department
West Midlands County Council

New Oscott College

Just a few miles over the border of the West Midlands County is Maxstoke Castle. The castle was built by Sir William de Clinton in 1346. Its history indicates that Richard III slept there on the eve of The Battle of Bosworth and that Henry VII slept in the same room the following night!

The castle is said to be haunted by the ghost of Mary Ward Dilke who died there in 1728 after falling down the stairs during a violent quarrel with her husband.

Grimshawe Hall, a mid-sixteenth century house at Knowle is believed to be haunted by the spirit of Frances, a young women who was murdered by a jealous lover after she had been escorted to a ball by another man. She was murdered in a bedroom known as the 'Haunted Chamber' and the phantom has been seen in and around the house dressed entirely in white.

Wychall Farm which once stood in Pope's Lane, King's Norton was believed to be haunted by the ghost of a previous owner, Miss Smout. Lieutenant Colonel Pickering, a Birmingham University lecturer who took rooms at the farm in 1935 saw the spectre on three separate occasions during that year and he was able to give a clear description which exactly fitted that of the late Miss Smout.

HIGHWAY MEN AND FOOTPADS

Highwaymen and footpads, when caught, were usually hanged by the roadside and their bodies left to hang on the gallows to deter others of like mind.

The ghost of a highwayman who was hanged and gibbetted at Chester Road, Sutton Coldfield is said to haunt the spot where Oscott College now stands. Sutton Park is believed to be haunted by

The Warwick Road at Knowle. A coach was stopped there in the late eighteenth century. The ghost of the driver, murdered by the footpads has been seen there on numerous occasions.

THE HAUNTED HEAD OF WALMLEY

In 1745 an advance party of an army under the command of The Duke of Cumberland, who were in pursuit of Bonnie Prince Charlie, happened upon a young man near The Tyburn House, Erdington. This poor unfortunate was not able adequately to answer their questions because of a severe speech defect. Angered by this and inflamed with drink the soldiers decided that he must be a spy and he was shot. Not content with this the drunken party severed the head from the body and, after throwing the body into a ditch, carried the head to New Shipton Farm, Walmley where it was thrown into an oak tree.

the ghost of Tom King, a highwayman who was burned to death for his crimes. A victim of highway robbery haunts

New Shipston Farm

In 1827 the tree was felled and the skull discovered. No-one knows the identity of this poor youth but it is believed that his 'head' still haunts that area of Wylde Green Road and Eachelhurst Road, looking for its body.

Less than a mile away at Penn's Lane, Walmley another ghost has been recorded. This phantom, in the form of a young woman in a taffeta dress, has been linked with the brutal rape and murder of Mary Ashford whose body was found there in 1817.

THE MURDER OF MARY ASHFORD

Mary Ashford of Erdington was just twenty years old when she was viciously violated and murdered and her death and the subsequent trial and acquittal of the man accused of her murder, Abraham Thornton, has been the subject of much speculation by theorists and criminologists. Sutton Coldfield Library has twenty seven books by various authors about this particular crime and trial. She lies buried in the churchyard at Holy Trinity Church and her gravestone bore the following warning.

'As a warning to Female Virtue
And a Humble Monument of
Female Charity
This stone marks the grave of
Mary Ashford
Who in the 20th Year
of her age,
Having incaustiously repaired
To a scene of amusement
Without proper protection,
Was brutally violated
and murdered
on the 27th May, 1817'.

An unlikely habitation for a ghost is a public telephone box in Station Road, Erdington. A ghostly woman who wears a pink cardigan and makes endless telephone calls has been seen there on several occasions.

The Haunted Telephone Box at Station Road, Erdington

OTHER FORMS OF HAUNTING

The ghosts of the West Midland County are not all in human form. a phantom lorry has terrified drivers on

the Coventry-Rugby Road and a phantom dog, black and of immense size has been reported at Sedgley and Wolverhampton.

Spring Heel Jack was a ghost which featured in stories of the industrial Black Country and in the lore of the Midland Canal folk. He was said to haunt the spoil heaps and cinder banks and was ascribed incredible athletic skills.

Rawhead and Bloody Bones were ghosts of old pit shafts and mine workings who would steal naughty children from their homes and take them to their dirty lairs. Many Black Country children were no doubt threatened into behaving themselves by their parents at the risk of being taken by these bogey men.

CHAPTER VII

Superstitions

WE MAY CONSIDER superstitions to be irrational, even absurd but in the pre-scientific world of our ancestors, who believed in the sacred nature of everyday things and their power of bestowing good or evil, their actions were rational. Rational or irrational there are many of us who touch wood, throw spilled salt over our shoulders, avoid the number thirteen and would never walk under a ladder, to avoid bad luck.

SIGNS AND OMENS IN EVERYDAY LIFE

The superstitions described in this chapter are known to have existed in The West Midlands County. Some are still practised others have been modified or changed with time.

Signs and omens abounded in everyday life from the beginning to the end of the day, even within the sanctity of one's home. It was unlucky to get into bed one one side and get out the other side; to do so was to ensure that nothing would go right that day. If one fell down the stairs it was good luck as long as there was no-one else on the staircase as it was bad luck to pass someone on the stairs. Should there be eggs for breakfast or in cooking, care should be taken in the disposal of the shells. On no account should they be burned as this would cause the hens to stop laying and dregs of milk slopped into the fire was sufficient to cause the cows to go dry.

THE SIGNIFICANCE OF BREAD, SALT AND KNIVES

Bread, because of its link with the Eucharist, was considered to be almost sacred and to throw it away or to burn it was certain to bring ill luck upon the family.

Salt has been used since time immemorial as a protection against evil and to spill it was a bad omen. It should never be scraped up but a little should be thrown over the left shoulder into the face of the Devil.

Knives, being made of steel, served as a protection against witchcraft and there are many 'knife' superstitions. To

45

cross knives at the table was a sign that there would be a quarrel unless they were immediately uncrossed. To spin a knife at the table was likely to cause bad luck as was using a knife to make toast. When a knife was given as a present something had to be given in exchange, usually a small coin. This was to prevent the severing of a friendship.

SQUEAKY SHOES

It was unlucky to put shoes on a table, especially if they were new, and unlucky to put the left shoe on first whilst dressing. Squeaky shoes were

said to indicate that the wearer hadn't paid for them. Black Country miners thought it a sign of impending disaster to dream of broken shoes.

It was lucky to put a garment on inside out as long as it was done accidently but it had to be worn that way to gain the luck. To mend clothes whilst wearing them was asking for bad luck.

Seven years bad luck following the breaking of a mirror is still a common belief as is the luck-bringing power of finding a horseshoe.

Clocks, being the instrument of measuring time, have long been assoc iated with men's lives. Unusual behaviour like the speeding of the tick, the clock striking thirteen or a clock starting without being wound was a death omen.

UNEXPLAINED BODY SENSATIONS

The unexplained body sensations which we experience from time to time such as itching, tingling or burning of the skin were thought to have special significance. Such a sensation occurring to the right side of the body generally indicated good fortune whilst the same sensation on the left foretold the opposite. If the right hand itched you would receive money but an itchy left hand would mean that you will be paying money out. If the sensation is to the right ear someone is talking kindly about you, if its the left ear someone is bearing you ill will. An itching right eye means the approach of a pleasant surprise but you will be disappointed if scratching your left eye.

If your cheeks burn someone is talking about you and if your nose itches be particularly careful. You could be kissed, vexed, cursed, squeezed against a gate post or shake hands with a fool!

That tiresome itch on the sole of the foot could mean that you will go somewhere where you have never been and if your knee itches you could kneel in a strange place.

An involuntary shiver was thought to indicate that someone has walked upon the shiverer's future grave.

SNEEZING SUPERSTITIONS

The custom of asking a blessing from God for a person who has just sneezed is an extremely ancient and widespread custom. In the seventeenth century it was customary to doff one's hat and to bow whilst pronouncing 'God bless you'. Sneezing superstitions have been

teeth, is a recent innovation. If birds carried away locks of hair for nest building the 'donor' would suffer terrible headaches.

Horses have been sacred since early times. They were the mode of transport of Gods and were a symbol of fertility. White horses could be lucky or sometimes unlucky. On seeing a white horse it was customary to spit and wish or cross one's fingers until a dog came into view. Piebald and skewbald horses, much favoured by gipsies, were lucky and a welcome sight.

recorded in Ancient Greek and Roman history and the number, time of day, and day of the week has always been significant:

> *'Monday for danger,*
> *Tuesday kiss a stranger*
> *Wednesday for a letter,*
> *Thursday something better,*
> *Friday for sorrow,*
> *Saturday see your love*
> *tomorrow'.*

Finger nails, toe nails and hair are the only parts of the human body which are cut away and discarded and nail and hair cutting have their own associated superstitions.

BAD DAYS FOR A HAIRCUT

If hair is cut when the moon is waning it will remain short, conversely the waxing moon will stimulate hair growth. It was not recommended that hair should be cut on Thursdays, Saturdays or Sundays and especially not on a Good Friday.

Nail parings, hair and teeth should be destroyed by fire so that fairies and witches could not use them in magic charms. The kind Tooth Fairy, who rewards little children for their milk

BIRDS OF ILL OMEN

Magpies and other birds which are black and white are sometimes lucky but more often unlucky. To see a solitary magpie is ill omened but the ill luck can be averted by bowing to it, spitting or crossing the fingers. Two magpies seen together were lucky but the spitting and bowing ritual was necessary to promote the good luck.

Pigeons or other birds flying against a window, down a chimney or into a room were death omens especially if there was an ill person in the house.

The cuckoo, which arrives in the Midlands in April, was considered to be a herald of good weather. To hear the cuckoo from the right or the front was good luck, the converse from the left. It added a little extra luck if money in the pocket or pouch was turned once together with a silent wish.

The screeching cry of the barn owl was widely believed to foretell death especially if the cry was heard during the daylight hours.

Robins are among the best loved of British birds and to kill or injure one or to steal a robin's egg was considered very stupid. The consequences could be prolonged sickness and to be in the power of witches or the Devil. Despite this to see a robin perched on a wall, a gate or a house, indeed anything man made, was a sign of disaster to the miners of the Black Country.

*It was unlucky to harm a Wren
or a Robin. To see a Robin perched on a
man-made object was also
thought to be unlucky.*

BEES CAN FORETELL THE FUTURE

Bees have always been regarded as wise, diligent, and to have the gift of foretelling the future. It was believed that the bees should be told of every important family event such as a birth, a marriage and especially the death of the bee master. The telling of the bees was done by the eldest son or the widow who knocked three times on the

*Bees were told of a death in the family.
This photograph is of a Skep Stand.*

hive with a door key and said, 'The master is dead!' If this was not done the bees would die or vacate the hive.

Black beetles, or 'black bats' the local name, were a sign of bad luck but it was unlucky to kill one; to do so guaranteed torrential rain.

Spiders were lucky and should never be killed and money spiders, the young of garden spiders, if treated kindly could bring future riches. A well known rhyme concerning the creature's welfare advises:

*'If you wish to live and thrive,
let the spider run alive'.*

House crickets too were considered lucky though white ones were death omens.

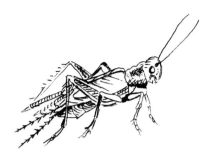

SACRED AND MAGICAL TREES

There are many superstitions associated with plants. Oak and ash trees were considered to have sacred and magical powers and to cut down either was considered bad luck. The oak which occasionally hosts mistletoe was especially revered. Those who wore the leaves of either tree were protected from evil and both trees were thought to be free from lightning strike and would safely provide shelter from a storm. Ash keys were used for magic charms to cure bed wetting and ear ache and 'even ash' leaves, those with an equal number of leaves to the stem, could be used in divination to foretell a future spouse.

Holly and ivy being evergreens were considered symbols of enduring life and if either were planted in a garden or against a house wall the occupants would be protected from witches, demons and lightning strike.

Elder wood was used in magic charms by witches and used by white witches against witchcraft. The leaves, bark, flowers and berries were used as remedies for various ills and the tree was also thought to protect against lightning. The timber was avoided as firewood and was unlucky to bring into the house.

A heavy crop of berries was believed to indicate the approach of a hard winter though, in truth, it is a result of a mild autumn and winter.

Oak and ash trees were used as indicators of the weather. In the unlikely event of an ash bearing leaves before an oak the summer would be wet. When, as is generally the case, the oak burst its buds first, the weather would be unsettled but less wet.

Broad beans were planted when elm leaves were as big as a shilling and kidney beans when the leaves were as big as a penny.

UNLUCKY AND LUCKY PEOPLE

A person's appearance or profession was sometimes significant in terms of good or bad luck. It was unlucky to meet a cross eyed person or a man with a wooden leg. To meet a chimney sweep, by chance, was very lucky especially at a wedding. The sweep must be soot encrusted and be walking towards the observer. In some areas he should be bowed to and it was customary to spit and wish for future good fortune.

It was lucky to meet a sailor and to touch his collar. In the land-locked

West Midlands, it was rare to see a sailor in uniform which made the encounter even luckier.

BOWING TO THE MOON

There were many moon superstitions. It was considered very unlucky to see the new moon through glass or trees and at all times a new moon was respectfully greeted with a bow or curtsy. A widespread practice was to turn the money in ones's pocket to ensure the good luck.

As the moon waxed or waned it affected all growing or changing things. Seeds were sown with the waxing moon; trees were pruned and eggs were set under broody hens to ensure a good hatch. As the moon waned it was wrong to dock lambs tails, to castrate animals and especially to kill a pig as the meat would shrink in the pot. To see the first star of the evening was lucky and a wish could be granted provided that the following rhyme was said:

'Star light, star bright
The first star I've seen tonight,
Would it were that I might
Have the wish I wish tonight'.

A shooting star seen on the right was lucky but to see one on the left spelt misfortune.

MAGIC CURES AND CHARMS

Healing charms and magic cures were handed down from one generation to the next and some are still practised especially in rural areas. Wart charmers were known for their skill in removing the ugly growths which were far more common then than present day. Other cures were rubbing them on nine successive days with the inside of a broad bean pod, dipping them in the blood of a recently killed pig or stroking the wart with cat's fur.

I remember being advised to steal a piece of meat, rub it on my warts and then bury it. As the meat decayed so would the warts. I also remember being told to count my warts, pick up the same number of stones and throw them away. With me the broad bean worked.

Chilblains were cured by soaking them in urine, cow dung or snow! Unpleasant but not so painful as thrashing them with holly leaves as was recommended in the South Staffordshire area of the West Midland County.

Rubbing
a Stye
with a
Wedding
Ring

Sties or powkes were removed by stroking them nine times on nine successive days with a wedding ring.

ROAST MOUSE CURE
FOR SNEEZING

In 1980 Trisha Ray, a Sutton Coldfield school girl was struck with a bout of continuous sneezing which lasted for weeks. Reports of Tricia's plight was published in the press and on local television and she became the record holder for non-stop sneezing in *The Guinness Book of Records*. The publicity prompted many people to write with local remedies the most common of which was to eat roast mouse. This is a well documented local cure for whooping cough, severe colds and bed-wetting. Tricia was eventually cured by a trip to a clinic in Switzerland which was financed by the *Sunday Mercury* 'Give a Girl Health Appeal.'

Rheumatism could be eased or cured by carrying the gall of a wild rose or a potato in a waistcoat pocket and a bleeding nose by putting a front door key down the patient's back.

TRANSFER OF ILLNESS TO PLANTS AND ANIMALS

The magical transfer of illness to plants and animals was commonly practised. Children suffering from whooping cough, known as chin cough, were given rabbits to play with. After a suitable time the rabbits were released taking the illness with them. Snails were also used as 'scape goats'. Bread and butter was given to the sick child and the scraps put into the garden for the snails.

Some of the charms were extremely cruel. Another cure for whooping cough, toothache and sore throat involved the severing of the forefeet of a live mole or toad and the patient wearing them around the neck. The mutilated creatures were released and as they died it was supposed the sickness would leave the child. Other cures and charms for childhood ailments are described in Chapter 1.

The touch of the hand of an executed felon was believed to cure anything from barrenness to rheumatism. Scrofula, a decease marked by the swelling of the lymphatic glands especially in the neck, was believed curable if touched by the hand of a monarch. It is recorded that in 1712 Dr. Johnson was taken to London to be touched by Queen Anne. A more common name for the complaint was King's Evil.

ADENOCHOIRADELOGIA:

OR,

An Anatomick - Chirurgical

TREATISE

OF

GLANDULES & STRUMAES,

Or Kings = Evil = Swellings,

Together with the

Royal gift of Healing,

Or Cure thereof by Contact or Impofition of Hands, performed for above 640 Years by our

Kings of *ENGLAND*,

Continued with their Admirable Effects, and Miraculous Events; and concluded with many Wonderful Examples of Cures by their Sacred Touch.

All which are fuccinctly defcribed

By *JOHN BROWNE*,

One of His Majefties Chirurgeons in Ordinary, and Chirurgeon of His Majefties Hofpital.

Si multitudo Sapientum (Confiliariorum) fanitas eft Orbis Terrarum, multò magis Rex Sapiens firmamentum ac Bafis Populi eft.

LONDON: Printed by Tho. Newcomb for Sam. Lowndes, over againft Exeter-Exchange in the Strand. 1684.

CHAPTER VIII

Games and Amusements

CHILDREN FOUND TIME, in spite of work and school, to play games. Many of these were imitations of grown up activities but others were games with strict rules and adherences.

French and English was an organised piggy-back fight between two teams. The first team to completely unseat the opposition were the victors. Rounders and Tut Ball were popular street games well into the twentieth century. Tut Ball was similar to rounders but the hand was used instead of a bat.

Hide and seek or 'Cuckoo' as it is known locally, was a popular childrens' game as was Stag Warning, a dodging, catching game involving many players.

The 'stag' tigged or ticked individuals who then linked hands with the stag and assisted him in chasing and cornering the others. The last to be caught became the new stag.

TIP CAT AND DOG STICK

Tip Cat was a simple game using easily made equipment. The 'cat' was a piece of wood, about six inches long and slightly sharpened on each end. The 'club' was a stout stick, roughly a yard long, though this could vary depending on the size of the players. The 'cat' was placed in the centre of a large circle and struck vertically with the club which forced it to rise into the air. The player with a second strike, then attempted to hit it out of the circle.

Dog Stick was a similar game but a hard, wooden ball was used instead of the cat. The object was to hit the ball as far as possible with a given number of strokes.

A game known as Nine Mens' Morris was popular especially in rural areas. Brand describes it as a game played on green turf or bare ground. A square varying in size from a foot square to three yards or more was cut in the turf and a smaller square with its sides parallel to the larger and joined to it by diagonal lines connecting the angles and straight lines connecting the middle of sides. One team playing with wooden pegs, the other with stones, tried to capture the other teams 'men' in a sort of chess game. Those captured were placed in the centre square which was known as 'the pound'. Each team had nine players.

TIT, TAT, TOW AND IN A ROW

The Black Country version called 'Tit, tat, tow and in a Row' was played by two players. This was played on a board marked into nine squares and each player attempted to place three counters on a line; similar to Noughts and Crosses.

A game similar to conkers was played using cobnuts and J. Harvey Bloom describes a game called 'Conqueror' using snail shells. Each contestant would press his shell against that of his opponent in an attempt to crush it. A shell that was successful in crushing many shells or crushing an established 'Conqueror' became a much prized possession.

BEGGING A BARLEY

There are periods in strenuous games when a player needs a respite. This is not surrender but just a chance to take

Begging a 'Barley'

off a coat, tie a shoe lace or rest a 'stitch'. The truce term used in The West Midland County was, and still is, 'Barley'.

To beg a 'barley' is an extremely ancient way of asking for a respite or rest. It is recorded in the Fourteenth Century poem *Sir Gawayne and the Grene Knight*.

> *'And I shall stonde hym a strok*
> *Stif on this flet*
> *Elles thou wil dight me the*
> *dom-to del him another Barley*
> *And yet fif him reespite*
> *A twelmonth and a day'.*

There are nine main truce territories in great Britain and 'Barley' is by far the most common.

GAMES FOR THE HUMBLE CLASSES

Most of the afore mentioned games were played without special equipment or with equipment which was readily made but Hutton relates that: 'The relaxations of the humbler classes are fives, quoits, skittles and ale'. He records that there were facilities for the use of the public to bowl or play quoits at The Cross at Vauxhall and The Plough and Harrow at Edgbaston. *(The History of Birmingham* 1835).

Other games of skill or chance included billiards, cards, dominoes, bagatelle, marbles, and cricket in the summer.

Shovel Board, a game which consisted of 'shoving' or pushing with nail or finger, a coin along a polished surface to a given spot, was introduced to this country by Henry VIII. His four pence piece or groat was known as a 'shove groat'. A nine foot table is preserved at Maxstoke Castle. The game, known as Shove Half Penny was revived this century and was played in pubs until it was outlawed by a gambling act.

CRUEL SPORTS
WERE VERY POPULAR

Dog fights, badger drawing and bear baiting were popular sports. Bear baiting was less common, presumably because of the availability of bears, but a famous bear 'Old Nell' was baited weekly in a yard in Coleshill Street.

Birmingham's famous Bull Ring became a venue for the cruel sport of bull baiting when permission was granted by Henry VIII. In 1773 a law was passed which banned bull baits from the streets of Birmingham but they persisted long afterwards in private yards and on private land. Birmingham was said to be the most notorious place in England for this cruel sport and bull baits remained a feature of most holidays and wakes with the last recorded event being in 1838.

Several people would 'club' together to buy a suitable animal. Once procured the poor beast was tethered to a stake and selected dogs were set upon it. As the dogs became exhausted or wounded they were replaced and it was not uncommon for a bull to endure this torment for three or four consecutive days. Occasionally a bull broke loose and ran amock amongst the spectators. *The Birmingham Gazette* September 6th 1790 records that:

'On Tuesday evening a bull that was being baited near Gosta Green broke loose from the stake and though he threw many people and ran into a house in Aston Street, where there was a poor woman and child, very fortunately no serious injury was done to anyone'.

There were many dissenters who wrote to the press expressing their revulsion to these cruel practices. *The Aris Gazette* October 8th 1792 printed the following letter.

'A correspondent laments, with some degree of astonishment, that in this neighbourhood (so distinguished for its charitable institutions) a custom so barbarous as that of Bull Baiting should still have continuance among the common people.

Surely cruelties of this kind may be prevented, by refusing those particulars a licence who either procure the animal (which is sometimes the case) or who supply with liquor the unfeeling rabble who assemble to enjoy the horrid amusement'.

Dent records an incident in 1798 when a body of 'Volunteer Militia formed by a trading class' rescued a bull which was scheduled for a bait behind The Salutation Inn, Snow Hill. The animal was locked in the yard of the old prison, Peck Lane, where it survived an attempt to release it during the night.

Cock fighting was extremely popular. W. Hutton writes: 'The announcements of such events to come off are more numerous than those of any kind except, perhaps, the theatre'.

One such announcement in June 1746 read:

'This is to give notice — that there will be a Main of Cocks fought at Duddeston Hall, near Birmingham, betwixt the Gentlemen of Warwickshire and Worcestershire, for four guineas a battle and forty guineas the Main. To weigh on Monday 9th June, and fight the two following days'.

A 'main' was a series of matches fought in a pit or ring approximately

The Cock-Pit at Avoncroft Museum

twenty two feet in diameter surrounded by a low wall. Some of the cock fighting jargon for different weight categories (eg. feather weight, bantam weight) has been transferred to boxing.

Throwing at Cocks was another cruel activity which was indulged in, especially on Shrove Tuesday. This activity usually took place out of doors in a field or yard. A stake was driven into the ground and a cockerel tethered

to it, by one leg, with a ten foot length of cord. Another post was driven in twenty paces distant which acted as the thrower's mark. The projectiles were lengths of wood about a yard long with a diameter of one and a half inches. If the thrower could knock the bird over and catch it before it recovered he kept is as a prize. The cost was two pence for three throws.

PUBLIC OPINION ENDED BLOOD SPORTS

Public opinion against blood sports gained momentum in the late eighteenth century and early nineteenth century and cock fighting was banned under the Cruelty to Animals act of 1849. This saw the end of large public matches but private fights were staged in back street public houses until much later. A Birmingham publican was fined £5 in 1868 for allowing his premises to be used for cock fighting and the sport is said to have continued at The White Lion, Digbeth well into the 1870's. Cock fights, dog fights and badger baits are still staged at secret locations; ten men were charged with staging a dog fight, in Birmingham on the 27th November 1990.

PRIZE FIGHTING TAKES OVER

With the almost total elimination of brutal animal sports attention was turned to 'man fights'. Birmingham was considered the provincial centre for prize fighting and pugilists of national fame such as Bob Brettle, Ben Count and Hammer Lane learned their craft in the back streets of the city.

These fights were not split into three minute rounds with a scheduled number of rounds as in present day

boxing. A round ended with a knock-down and the fight ended when a contestant failed to come to the 'scratch' at the beginning of a new round. The contests were particularly brutal and many fighters suffered heavy punishment for long periods, in some cases as long as two or three hours.

Monday was the most popular day for staging prize fights. This was due to the long established local custom of taking a holiday on Monday in honour of 'St Monday'. The sport envoked rowdyism and drunkenness amongst the spectators and was the main cause of it being banned by the police and it had all but disappeared by the mid-nineteenth century.

THEATRE AND MUSICAL HALL GAINS POPULARITY

Live theatre, in the form of travelling players who staged their performances in inn yards, market squares and other public places, was always popular. The

first theatre to be opened in Birmingham was the *New Theatre* in Moor Street in 1740 and the first purpose built theatre, *The Theatre,* King Street, eleven years later.

Music halls were, in effect, working mens' theatres. These originated in public houses, often in special rooms set aside for the purpose. They were extremely popular and presented 'turns' of great variety and ingenuity. Public houses, which were open all day, were the great social centres where music hall turns, games such as dominoes, cards, skittles, marbles and quoits could be enjoyed.

THE CURSE OF DRINK

Drunkenness was a major social problem in Victorian Birmingham. In 1869 there were recorded 2187 Drunk and Disorderly cases — roughly 1 in 70 of the population. Drunkenness and rowdy behaviour led to the demise of wakes and fairs. Church wakes were watch services on the eve of the feast of Dedication when people attended late night services at their local church. In Birmingham there were three principal wakes.

The Deritend Wake, commemorating the erection of St John's Chapel in 1381 was held on the 29th August. The Chapel Wake in commemoration of the completion of St Bartholomew's Chapel in 1750 and The Bell wake, held on the 24th August, marked the hanging of ten bells in St Philip's Church 1751.

Though respectable in origin the devotional aspect was soon forgotten and each wake became an excuse for the watching of cruel sports, drunkenness and debauchery.

THE ONION FAIR

The two foremost Birmingham fairs were the Onion Fair and The Whitsun Fair. The Whitsun Fair, dating from 1251 when William de Birmingham obtained a charter from Henry III, was held on the Thursday of Whitsun week and lasted for four days. The Onion Fair was traditionally held on 29th of September and became known as The Onion Fair because it attracted onion growers from Buckinghamshire.

The show tents were pitched in the inner city streets with most of the

activities designed for pleasure. *The Birmingham Post,* of 1874, lists, 'cake, gingerbread and toy stalls, peep shows, art studios. swinging boats, shooting galleries, instruments for the trial of strength and menageries. Other attractions included waxworks, conjurers, giants, dwarves, fat women and animal monstrosities.

An anti-fair lobby, which included industrialists and moralists, campaigned vigoriously against the siting of the fairs and in 1875 the City Council prohibited the use of the streets for fairs. The traders moved to Aston where the Onion Fair was continued until the 1950's.

Mop or Hiring fairs were usually held in the autumn and were sometimes combined with a trade fair. Farm lads and maid servants assembled at these fairs and offered themselves for hire for the following year. They sometimes wore the badge of their trade and the word 'mop' is thought to be derived from the wearing of miniature mops by house maids.

Coventry had fairs on the second Sunday in Lent, for the sale of cloth, the 2nd May and in June there were eight days of the 'fun of the fair' which included the famous Procession of Lady Godiva. The final fair of the year was 2nd of November for the sale of cloth and horses.

The Wolverhampton Wool Fair began on the 9th July, Brierley Hill held a wake on 29th September and an annual horse fair was held at Wednesbury during October.

The Bandstand in Aston Park, circa 1900

THE START OF
PRESENT DAY RECREATION

By the late nineteenth century sport and recreation activities had changed and were more in keeping with the present day. Swimming baths, public parks, museums, art galleries and libraries were opened to the general public. Gardening was a popular pastime for those fortunate enough to have a garden or an allotment and reading was very much enjoyed by those who had benefitted from schooling.

The two Birmingham association football clubs, Aston Villa (1874) and Birmingham City (1875) evolved within

twelve months of each other and marked the beginning of commercially organised sport. The Warwickshire Cricket Club made Birmingham its home ten years later in 1885.

WARWICKSHIRE ELEVEN, 1886.

F. COLLISHAW.   H. O. WHITBY.   LORD WILLOUGHBY   G. H. CARTLAND.   A. LAW.
DE BROKE.

H. PALLETT.   E. WHEELER.   W. G. MICHELL.   J. E. SHILTON.   C. ALLEN.   J. GRUNDY.

———— • • • ————

CHAPTER IX

Stories and Legends

LEGENDS ARE POPULAR stories handed down from earlier times whose truth have not been ascertained. The stories in this chapter are legends, traditional local literature based on fact. Three of the stories are about legendary characters but the first is a folk story about an ancient local object, the Gilbertstone.

More than a million years ago, a huge boulder fell from a glacier in that district of Birmingham we now call Sheldon. No-one knows from whence it came but for hundreds of years it was used as a boundary marker where the parishes of Sheldon, Bickenhill and Yardley met. This was also the boundary between Warwickshire and Worcestershire until 1911. Known as The Gilbertstone, it now rests in the grounds of historic Blakesley Hall at Yardley and is the subject of a legend from the Middle Ages.

THE GILBERTSTONE

Long ago Birmingham was a little market town surrounded by small farms and scattered forests. On such a farm, on a hilltop, five miles to the east of the town, lived a man called Gilbert. Though Gilbert's land was poor he made a reasonable living from his crops, his sheep and cows. He was however a greedy man and was envious of his neighbour Jacob, whose land bordered his.

Jacob's land was rich. It grew fine grass and his animals were sleek and well fed. One field was particularly fertile. It bordered Gilbert's land and he would often sit on the great boundary stone and wish that this fine meadow was his. He decided to save as much silver as he could to buy the land and after scrimping and saving for some considerable time he managed to fill a small leather bag with coins and visited Jacob to make his offer.

Though Jacob and Gilbert were close neighbours they were not friends and Gilbert was surprised when Jacob invited him into his house and gave him refreshment. When he suggested that Jacob might sell him the field for the bag of silver Jacob refused. Jacob did indicate however that he would exchange the land for the silver plus a small wood which Gilbert owned which was full of fine oaks that he knew could command a fine price.

Gilbert was no fool. He knew the value of those giant trees so, with a grunt of disgust, he repouched the silver and stalked out of the house. Arriving once again at the boundary stone, he rested deep in thought. He was a man of great strength and he decided that, under the cloak of darkness, he would attempt to move the stone further down the hill.

As soon as darkness fell, armed with a heavy pole, he slunk to the great stone and tried to lever it down the hill. The sweat of his brow glistened in the moonlight as he struggled in vain until he collapsed to the ground.

Blakesley Hall, Yardley

The Gilbertstone

A HOBGOBLIN APPEARED

As he lay confused and exhausted a strange hollow chuckle broke the stillness. Gilbert looked towards the stone and saw the silhouette of a small figure with bright piercing eyes, huddled on its top. The hobgoblin, for

that is what the apparition was, introduced himself to the trembling farmer and offered to move the stone in exchange for the right to live in Gilbert's wood.

Gilbert wanted the field so badly that he would have done a deal with the Devil, so he agreed to leave every tree intact.

The following morning Gilbert found that the great stone had been moved leaving no trace of the previous boundary. Within the hour Jacob and a group of villagers arrived and accused Gilbert of moving the stone but Gilbert laughed them to scorn pointing out the absence of bruised grass and fresh soil. They reluctantly agreed.

Gilbert became even more greedy. A timber merchant, who was visiting the farm to remove a fallen apple tree admired the timber in the wood and valued it at ten gold sovereigns. Quickly forgetting his promise to the hobgoblin Gilbert allowed one tree to be felled and promised the merchant more timber later.

Gilbert's luck changed. As soon as the oak tree was loaded onto the merchant's waggon a wheel came off and the tree rolled down the hill and into the river and was lost without payment.

Stones appeared all over his land. He broke his scythe so his harvest was late and damp. His corn stack caught fire and was burned to ashes and worst of all, the boundary stone inexplicably returned to its original spot.

Gilbert was ruined because of his greed.

Where Gilbert's farm once stood there are now houses, shops and schools but Hob's little wood remains and the legend lives on in the local street names — Gilbertstone Avenue, Hob's Moat and Hob Moor Road.

THE LEGEND OF LADY GODIVA

The story of Lady Godiva, who rode naked through the streets of Coventry to free the people from burdensome taxes, is probably the most famous midland legend. Whether or not she actually rode naked through the town has been a matter of discussion by local historians but the legend has survived for more than eight hundred years.

There is no doubt that Lady Godiva did exist. She is mentioned in *The Domesday Book* as a rich Warwickshire landowner and it is known that she died in 1067. Her husband Leofric, Earl of Mercia, ruled a great deal of the English midlands. There is no evidence that they lived in Coventry or of their marriage but their names were linked in 1035. They certainly endowed an abbey at Coventry and were responsible for other benefactions.

PEEPING TOM — A MYTH?

Peeping Tom is not mentioned in writing until the seventeenth century and is considered by the experts to have been added to the story by the seventeenth century historian Paul de Rapin. There is no contemporary evidence that he ever existed.

The earliest account of the ride is by Roger of Wendover, history writer to the Abbey of St. Albans, written sometime between 1188 and 1237.

'The countess Godiva, a true lover of the Mother of God, longed to free the town of Coventry from heavy bondage and servitude, and often with urgent prayers begged her husband, that out of regard for Jesus Christ and His Mother, he would free the town of that service and from all other heavy burdens.

The Earl constantly refused and sharply rebuked her for asking what was so much to his damage and forbade her evermore to speak to him again on the matter.

Godiva however with womanly pertinacity never ceased to worry her husband on that matter until at last he answered and said, "Mount your horse naked, and ride through the market of the town from the beginning to the end when the people are assembled, and when you return, you will have what you ask."

To which Godiva, replying said, "And if I am willing to do this will you grant me leave?"

"I will," he said.

Then the Countess, cherished of God, attended by two soldiers, as is said before, mounted her horse naked, letting down the hair and tresses of her head so that her whole body was veiled except for her very beautiful legs, and no one saw her as she traversed the market place. The journey completed, she returned to her husband rejoicing and he, filled with admiration, freed the town of Coventry, and its people, from servitude and confirmed it by his charter."

Lady Godiva processions began in 1678 and continued up to the last war with actors dressed in various tight fitting clothes so as to appear naked. They were not always looked upon favourably and in 1848 the bishop wrote to the mayor expressing disfavour. In 1962, Cathedral Festival Year, a procession was held with Mrs Joyce Parker playing the part of Lady Godiva.

A statue of Lady Godiva by Sir William Reid Dick stands in the city centre and 'Godiva's Prayer' a painting by Landseer was a gift to Coventry by Mr Bassett-Green.

BISHOP VESEY

In 1462 a son was born to William Harman a Sutton Coldfield yeoman. The boy was christened John. He was a fine scholar and after graduating from Oxford began a career in the church. He was later to become tutor to Princess Mary, friend of Cardinal Wolsley, close associate of Henry VIII and Bishop of Exeter. At some unknown time and for some unknown reason he took the name of Vesey.

Bishop Vesey loved his native town and became its most famous benefactor. He revived its ancient fairs and markets, paved the town, built bridges at Water Orton and Curdworth, built houses for the poor and endowed the grammar school known as Bishop Vesey's Grammar School. By his considerable influence in high places he was also able to bring to an end the fuedal system, in Sutton Coldfield with the introduction of fixed rents.

Rogues, beggars and layabouts were rounded up by the Bishop's men and put to work clearing stones from the roads for which they were paid a small wage. He also brought looms and weavers from Devon and tried unsuccessfully, to introduce the craft of weaving to the town.

The story 'The Bishop's Wager' is adapted from a nineteenth century story.

The Bishop's Wager

Good food, a warming drink, a roaring fire, a sturdy house to keep out the icy wintery weather and peace and

The Farmhouse, Moor Hall, supposed birthplace of Bishop Vesey

Bridge across the River Cole at Water Orton

quiet. Bishop Vesey felt content as he dined alone in his moated house at Moor Hall. It was mid-day yet the room was dark. The small mullioned windows, partly boarded up for winter, afforded very little light but the cheerful glow from the fire was sufficient for his needs.

The Bishop looked up from his meal as he heard footsteps on the spiral stone staircase which led from the ground floor to his apartments. There was a knock at the door and a liveried servant entered and stood nervously dangling his red cap in his hands.

"Well speak up man", prompted his master, "what business is important enough to interrupt my meal?"

"If it please your Lordship, Richard Hodgkin says he'll gather no more stones off the road today," stammered the servant.

INSUBORDINATION FROM SWEARING DICK

Such a piece of rank insubordination was unheard of in Moor Hall and from Dick Hodgkin too, a lazy uncouth individual known locally as 'Swearing Dick'.

"Which road is Richard doing?" asked the Bishop.

"He's cleaning the hill down by the brook, just by the moat, may it please your Lordship."

"Then send him to me at once."

The servant left and soon heavy footsteps echoed on the staircase. The door opened and Richard entered and stood, looking quite relaxed, with both thumbs tucked into his belt.

Vesey was warming his hands at the fire and for a few moments remained in the same position, apparently deep in thought, then rousing himself suddenly rounded and glared at Swearing Dick. The look would have been enough to wither a lesser man but Dick remained perfectly at ease with a defiant smile on his unshaven face.

"Richard, what's this I hear? You refuse to gather stones? Now listen to me, don't think my friendship for you will cause me to spare you one jot of your fair share of work. You may not like it but I know you to be a lazy and ungrateful fellow. How such an honest and hardworking man can father such an idle son amazes me. I've known your father man and boy sixty years and more and I have never known him be idle for an hour. Now he holds the honourable position of parish sexton. Richard you'll never live to match that".

"No I'll be buried first!"

"You are nothing but a thankless, arrogant knave. It's the likes of you that fill our stocks and pillories. I'll be surprised if you escape the gallows. It's not the first time that I've tried to help you. Did I not have a stone house built for you? Did I not bring a loom all the way from Exeter and fit it for you? But still you wouldn't work".

"It was the loom that wouldn't work", Dick interrupted.

"No Richard, remember the old saw . . ."

"Yes that loom did sound like an old saw", he interrupted once again.

"You were never able to curb that tongue of yours", the Bishop corrected, "I was telling of the old saw, 'the bad workman always blames his tools', and now when I try to find you employment on the road you refuse to gather more stones."

"I don't refuse", said Dick, "I can't".

"You won't out of sheer laziness an stubbornness. Oh I can see you coming to a bad end Richard. Now get back and clear that stretch of road, or by my faith, I'll have you whipped."

"Whip away Bishop, I tell you I can't do it," Dick scowled defiantly.

"Curb your tongue! You always were a saucy rascal and were it not for the sake of your father I'd have you flogged for your impudence. I'll give you one more chance to clear the stones off the hill."

The Bishop composed himself, paused and straightening himself looked Dick squarely in the eyes. "Why I've seen the time, and not long ago either, when I could have cleared it myself in an hour".

"I'm the strongest man in Sutton and I couldn't clear it in a week," Dick growled.

The Bishop was very proud of his physical fitness and Dick knew it. In his younger days he had been a veritable Samson and even now, though well on in years, he was very fit and strong.

"You couldn't do it in a week?" scoffed the Bishop. "Now look here Richard Hogdkin, as an example to you of energy in an old man and humility in a bishop, I have a mind to clear that road myself, and I'll do it in an hour!"

"It can't be done", Dick said, "I'll bet you don't clear it in a week Bishop. If you do it in an hour, I'll promise to clear the road between here and Bassett's Pole, however long it takes me. You can string me up if I don't."

"I'm not in the habit of wagering but to teach you a lesson I accept your challenge and you will see, that old as I am, I will make short work of it. There are but a few stones on the hill. They are not very heavy and have only to be moved to the bottom near the brook."

"Yes I know that", said Dick with a knowing grin, "but its all froze as hard as the devil's forehead and you can't move those stones with a crowbar".

The Bishop forgetting about the hard frost of the previous night was momentarily taken aback but soon recovered himself and with a stern glance at Dick he said, "Frozen it may have been, but it's not freezing now. Let's to the moat and see."

He rose, entered an ante-room and after a few moments returned with a warm cloak around his shoulders and with no further discourse led the way down the stairs and out towards the moat. The ground was frozen but the dark water showed the merest feathers of floating ice upon it.

"So this is the road that you claim I cannot clear of stones in an hour?" said the Bishop, standing by the side of the moat and looking down at the street below.

"That's it Bishop, and you won't clear those stones in a week if it keeps on freezing", Dick smirked.

NEVER WAGER WITH A BISHOP!

Without another word Vesey went to the old wooden floodgates, examined them carefully, and then producing a massive key from beneath his cloak he undid the lock and rusty chains which held the gates in position. Dick looked on silently in open mouthed wonderment and then a sympathetic smile spread over his face. "Must have been

A Vesey Cottage

drinking", muttered Dick to himself, "he'll fall in the moat next and I shall have to fish him out."

Vesey continued to remove the chains and as he removed the last one the water burst forth in a torrent and cascaded down the hill carrying all before it.

When the rush of water had subsided and he could make himself heard once more, the Bishop, looked at Dick with an amused smile and said, "Richard you are a strong and impudent young man but take an old man's advice and in future never wager with a bishop."

Dick was still too dazed to speak. He took off his cap and scratched his rough head, whilst he gazed at what had been the stony road but which now was swept clean of stones and everything else. "Well string me up if he ain't loosed the moat. No I'll never wager with a bishop again; hanged if I do."

———— •‌•‌• ————

SIR THOMAS HOLTE ACCUSED OF MURDER!

Aston Hall stands on high ground overlooking the main road to Lichfield and the Aston Expressway. This magnificent house was built by Sir Thomas Holte (1571—1654) who lived there from 1631 to his death in 1654. It is believed that he was a vindictive, relentless man who not only attempted to dis-inherit his eldest son Edward for marrying a lady not of his own liking but was also accused of murdering his cook with a cleaver. The alleged crime occurred in 1606 at Duddeston Manor where Sir Thomas Holte resided before moving to Aston Hall.

Sir Thomas's temper was known throughout the manor and was often directed at his numerous servants. He was however, very fond of good food and drink which was prepared and served to Sir Thomas and his guests in copious quantities by his head cook. This cook was not only skilled in the culinary arts but was also remarkably punctual in serving the victuals — so punctual indeed that Sir Thomas often boasted about it to his friends.

One day Sir Thomas, his lawyer Richard Smallbrooke and other friends were on a hunting trip some miles from Duddeston Hall. Holte was in a particularly sullen mood and, hoping to cheer him a little Smallbrooke challenged him to wager his cook's punctuality against his own best horse.

Holte accepted the challenge, never doubting his faithful servant but, on arrival at the Hall found him on this occasion to be unprepared. Inflamed with anger by the taunts of Smallbrooke and the others he seized a cleaver and 'cleft his skull in twain'.

Sir Thomas was acutely affected by the charge which was subsequently levelled against him and brought an

Aston Hall

action of slander against William Ascrick, one of his neighbours who claimed that:

> "Sir Thomas tooke a cleaver and hytt hys cooke with the same cleaver uppon the heade, and clave his heade, that on one syde thereof fell uppone one of his shoulders, and the other syde on the other shoulder: and this I will veryfie to be trewe".

The case reached the Court of the King's Bench, where judgement was in favour of Ascrick but the damages were reduced on the grounds that the defendant had not claimed the blow to be fatal! Holte did not deny the charge and there does appear to be a strong probability that the cruel murder was commited as Ascrick had testified.

———— •••• ————

CHAPTER X

A Calendar of Customs

JANUARY

A Good Fat Pig to last you all the Year

THE LAST STROKE of the clock at midnight (31st December — 1st January) signifies the beginning of a new year.

First footing or letting in the New Year was practised all over the West Midland County. It was considered unlucky to leave the house on January 1st until a dark haired man or boy had entered the house and wished the residents 'a happy New Year'. The rhyme or song which accompanied letting in the new year varied a little from district to district but it was usual to wish the incumbents a merry Christmas, a happy new year, a pocket full of money, a cellar full of beer, and a 'good fat pig to last you all the year'.

In rural areas church bells were rung and the wassail bowl passed around. In industrial areas the bells were often accompanied by works' sirens.

COVENTRY'S GOD CAKES

In Coventry on New Year's Day it was customary to eat God Cakes. These were triangular pastries filled with mince-meat.

Colliers throughout the region refused to work on New Year's Eve or New Year's Day and it was considered unlucky for the fire to go out between twelve noon on the last day of the year and twelve noon the following day.

From the sixteenth century to the early nineteenth century each person who lived in Walsall was given a small loaf of bread or a penny. This dole, distributed on Twelfth Eve, was bestowed by Thomas Moseley of Bascote Manor and was known as the Moseley Dole.

All Christmas decorations had to be taken down by Twelfth Night — to leave them up was unlucky.

Plough Monday, the first Monday after Twelfth Day, was considered the first day of the farming year.

FEBRUARY

A Time to Choose your Sweetheart

The weather on February 2nd, Candlemas Day, could signify the continuation of or the end of winter. If fair and bright winter continued, if wet and windy winter was over.

Saint Valentine's Day, 14th February, is traditionally the day when birds and

people chose their sweethearts. It was a great time for giving presents, often anonymously, but by the nineteenth century these gifts had become cards.

Shrove Tuesday, the day before Lent begins, was a day for a final fling. Pancakes were eaten and pancake races were popular and still are. In some parishes the Pancake Bell was rung at 11

a.m. to signify that it was time to prepare the batter. The first three pancakes were marked with a cross,

sprinkled with salt to ward off evil spirits, and not eaten. The season for street games of all sizes began on Shrove Tuesday; Tip cat, marbles, skittles and hop skotch were but a few.

Street football was also a feature of Shrove Tuesday. These were wild, all rules barred affairs with the teams comprising of hundreds of players from a particular parish or part of a town. The object was to get the ball from a given spot into the opponents' territory.

Cruel sports such as dog fighting, badger drawing, cock fights and 'throwing at cocks' were staged until outlawed last century.

MARCH

Apprentices visit their Mothers

The fourth Sunday in Lent usually occurs about the middle of March and is known as Mothering Sunday. This Mid-Lent Sunday was originally set aside as the day when the people of the parish visited the Mother Church. By the mid seventeenth century it had also become a day for visiting one's own mother. It was the only day when apprentices and 'living in' servants could get to see their mothers, taking them a bunch of primroses or violets picked on the way and sometimes a Simnell cake. This was a spicey cake whose origin is uncertain. It could be from the Latin 'simila', the fine wheat flour used in the baking of this cake.

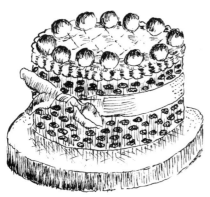

Simnel Cake

A traditional food for the day was frumenty which was made of boiled wheat grains, with milk, sugar and sometimes plums added. A Black Country substitute was dried, grey peas boiled with bacon.

Mothering Sunday, usually the second Sunday in May, is an American import dating from the last war.

APRIL

The Customs of Easter

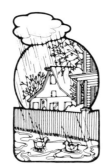

April 1st or All Fools' Day is one of the customs which is still practised. Practical jokes and pranks are tolerated until 12 noon.

Palm Sunday, the Sunday before Easter, was the day that Jesus rode into Jerusalem along a road strewn with palm leaves. Palms are not indigenous to the English Midlands and local church goers collected hazel, box, yew and especially pussy willows the catkins of the goat willow, as substitutes.

Most April customs surround Easter. Good Friday was the day when gardening began in earnest and was always taken as a holiday. Whilst the men and boys toiled in the gardens the women and girls baked bread and hot cross buns which were eaten for afternoon tea.

On Easter Sunday everyone wore new clothes for good luck and the churches were decorated with spring flowers and foliage. It was traditional for the children of the parish to 'clip the church'.

Clipping the Church

They stood with their backs to the church wall and linked hands until the building was totally surrounded. When the last child was in place the children

72

*St Martin's
in the
Bull Ring*

sang the hymn 'Round about thy temple Lord'. This was followed by tea and buns at their schoolroom. (Recorded at St. Martin's and St. Philip's churches in the mid nineteenth century).

Pace-egging was a common Easter custom. Young men and women, in various guises, visited the well-to-do and begged gifts of eggs, cakes and money. In some areas, notably The Mounts at Wednesbury, young people would roll eggs down grassy slopes, a symbol of the rolling away of the stone from the sepulchre on the first Easter Day.

Easter Monday and Tuesday were 'Heaving or Lifting Days'. Between 9 a.m. and 12 noon on Monday the men 'heaved the women', on the Tuesday the roles were reversed. This involved lifting the victim into the air and kissing him or her. A silver forfeit could be paid to avoid the kiss. This popular custom was widely practised up to the beginning of this century.

On 23rd April, St. George's Day, a custom known as The Riding of St George was enacted in Coventry. A man mounted on a horse, representing the patron saint, rode through the streets accompanied by a woman known as Sabra who led a captive dragon.

MAY

Jack in the Green and His Wife

May 1st or May Day was a great day of celebration. Young men and women gathered spring blossom and greenery to decorate their houses and the local maypole.

A bower was constructed for the Queen of the May and there was music and dancing on the village green, especially Morris dancing. Mummers and hobby horse dancers welcomed in the spring with the chief characters being Jack-in-the-Green and his wife. These were accompanied by various dancers dressed as women and using long wooden spoons to collect money from the onlookers. It was traditional for the local chimney sweeps to be principal dancers.

Oak Apple Day, on the 29th May was another popular celebration. This was in memory of Charles II's triumphal entry into London after escaping from the Roundheads by hiding in a Warwickshire oak tree. (This was on 4th September). Houses were decorated with oak leaves and boughs and oak apples were won in hats or button holes. Children who forgot to wear oak leaves were pursued by their friends who stung their legs with nettles as a punishment. After the Restoration many of the May day celebrations were moved to Oak Apple Day.

Whitsun usually falls in May and was another festival to enjoy feasting, drinking, fairs and sports, much in the manner of May Day and Oak Apple Day.

JUNE

Beating the Bounds

Beating the Bounds took place during Rogationtide which was 3 days before Ascension Day and five weeks after Easter. Rogation is from the Latin 'rogare' which means to ask or beseech.

The boundaries of the parish were systematically toured by the priests and civic leaders who stopped periodically to listen to readings from the gospels and prayers to bless the crops. The readings were often made beneath oak trees and the trees became known as Gospel Oaks. One in Birmingham gave the name to that district which still bears the name.

The boundary markers were often not 'marks' at all but just features of the landscape. Small boys were sometimes beaten, dumped in ponds, thrown into nettle beds or had their bottoms bumped on one of other of these land-

marks so that their memories would be sharpened for next years Beating of the Bounds.

Mid-Summer's Eve, 23rd June, was believed to be the night when witches and evil spirits were most active and most malevolent. In the west of the West Midlands County which was South Staffordshire it was customary for the people to decorate their houses and to make bonfires to guard against the witchcraft and bonfires were also lit in the streets of Coventry.

Protection against witchcraft was guaranteed if fern seed was gathered, placed in a white handkerchief, and carried on one's person and girls who scattered fern seed on Mid-Summer's Eve might see a vision of their future husband.

JULY

Paying Tribute to St. Blaise

The Wolverhampton Wool Fair began on the 9th July. The privilege to hold the fair was granted in 1354 by Edward III. The fair attracted merchants from all over Britain and even from mainland European countries.

It was a grand affair with music, dancing and feasting and celebrations to pay tribute to St. Blaise, the patron saint of wool-combers. Scheduled for eight days it often lasted up to two weeks. By the end of the eighteenth century it had gained a reputation for rowdy, drunken behaviour and eventually became a pleasure fair.

St Swithin's Day, July 15th, was used as a marker for the first digging of new potatoes. It was also known by the saying that if it rains on the day it will rain for forty days:

'St Swithin's Day, if it do rain,
For forty days it will remain'.

AUGUST

Street Dancing Bank Holiday

Ceremonial dancing was performed on August Bank holidays in Walsall, Wednesbury and Wolverhampton up to the middle of the seventeenth century. A procession of be-ribboned dancers, carrying sticks or ropes decorated with ribbons, executed their figures as they moved through the streets.

August 1st or Lammas, was the day when the flocks of the community were taken to graze on the common land and were allowed to remain until Candlemas (Feb 2nd). It was also a festival which marked the beginning of the harvest when small loaves of bread were baked from the first ears of wheat and used for Holy Communion.

SEPTEMBER

The Devil's Nutting Day

September 21st was known as The Devil's Nutting Day and it was unlucky to gather nuts on that day.

September 29th or Michaelmas Day ended the farming year and started the season of Mops and Hiring Fairs (See Chapter 8). It was also the date of the Birmingham Onion Fair.

OCTOBER

The Month of the Mop Fair

Mops and Runaway Mops, where farm workers who were unhappy with their former employment could ply for employment elsewhere, were usually held in October. The fairs also provided an opportunity for the buying and selling of livestock especially sheep, geese and horses.

October 31st, Hallowe'en or All Hallows Eve, was the day when it was believed that the ghosts of the dead returned to Earth and that witches and other evil spirits were present.

It was a favourable time for young girls to attempt to reveal the name of a future husband. At Knowle, it has been recorded, that the winner of a game of apple bobbing should peel the apple and throw the parings over her shoulder. The shape of the peel on the ground could indicate the initials of a future spouse. This was also practised on St Clement's Day especially in the Wednesbury area.

NOVEMBER

The Tradition of Soul Cakes

November 1st is All Saints' Day and November 2nd All Soul's Day. Souling or singing soul songs, by the poorer classes at the doors of the better off, for which they received gifts of soul cakes, fruit, ale and money, was practised on both days. The cakes were often flat, round cakes and seed cakes were popular. These were especially baked for the event by the housewives. (18th to mid 19th centuries).

Guy Fawkes Day or Bonfire Night (November 5th) is one of the customs which is still widely practised. The preparation of the 'Guy' and the bon-

fire, and the 'Penny for the Guy' collections start weeks before the actual event and are often communal affairs. Traditional fare for the evening is potatoes and chestnuts roasted in the embers of the fire.

November 23rd is St Clement's day. This was another occasion when souling or 'Clementing' took place. The day was especially enjoyed by children who went about the streets singing and begging for the reward of food or small sums of money. The following couplet is an extract from a much longer rhyme:

> *'An apple, a pear,*
> *   a plum or a cherry*
> *Or anything else*
> *   to make us all merry'.*

DECEMBER

Handouts for the Poor

December 21st, St Thomas's Day, was an important day for the poor. It was on

this day that public doles were distributed. These were often financed by legacies which were distributed by the churches. It was the last chance for the poorer classes to ask for handouts before the Christmas celebrations and received these in the form of warm blankets, clothes, food and fuel as well as money.

Christmas Eve was a day of great activity. Homes and churches were decorated with holly, ivy, mistletoe and other evergreens. Food was prepared for the Christmas Day feast and in the evening carol singers, sometimes with a wassail bowl, went forth to visit each house in turn. The singers would ensure good luck for the household if they were admitted through the front door and let out the back. The traditional drink for the wassail bowl was sweet, spicey ale with roasted apples. This concoction was known locally as 'lamb-swool' and was also drunk on St Clement's Day and other occasions.

People throughout the region believed that farm animals knelt on Christmas Eve and that honey bees sang carols in memory of the baby Jesus.

Church bells ringing in Christmas at 12 mid-night indicated the birthday of Jesus and it was common for families to mark the occasion by singing a carol, drinking a toast and wishing the assembly a Merry Christmas.

Traditional food included boar's head, brawn, capons, game, beef, mutton, pork, plum pudding and mince pies which was washed down with ale and wine. In some parishes the very poor were treated to a Christmas Day lunch at the local vicarage.

Yule logs were traditionally burned on Christmas Day and the unburnt pieces were retained and stored until the following year when they were used to kindle that year's log.

Boxing Day was the day when parish poor boxes were opened and their contents distributed to the poor. It also became customary for small gifts to be given to servants and tradesmen on that day.

Holy Innocents' Day, 28th December, was considered the unluckiest day in the year. It is the day when the slaughter of the boy babies, by Herod is commemorated and people believed that anything started on that date would end in disaster.

Bibliography

Adkins M. E.	*Haunted Warwickshire*	1901
Bird V.	*Warwickshire*	1973
Bloom J. H.	*Folklore Old Customs and Superstitions in Shakespeare Land.*	1930
Burbidge	*Old Coventry and Lady Godiva*	1952
Burne C. S.	*Shropshire Folklore*	1883
Coleman S. T.	*Staffordshire Folklore*	1955
Dent R. K.	*Old and New Birmingham*	1878-80
Freeman J.	*Black Country Stories and Sketches*	1931
Green A.	*Phantom Ladies*	1977
Grice F.	*Folk Tales of the West Midlands*	1952
Griffiths S. A.	*Black Dots. Stories of the Midlands*	1943
Hackwood F. W.	*Staffordshire Customs, Superstitions and Folklore.*	1924
	A Collection of Newspaper Cuttings Relating to Warwickshire	1903-16
Hole C.	*The Encyclopedia of Superstitions*	1980
Hutton W.	*A History of Birmingham*	1835
Jones D. V.	*The Royal Town of Sutton Coldfield A Commemorative History*	1974
Langford J. A.	*Warwickshire Folklore and Superstitions*	1878
	A Century of Birmingham Life, Vols 1 and 2	1868
Lawley G. T.	*Staffordshire Customs, Superstitions and Folklore*	circa 1922
Lyons A.	*Black Country Sketches*	1901
Palmer R.	*The Folklore of Warwickshire*	1976
	Birmingham Ballads	1979
Plot R.	*The Natural History of Staffordshire*	1686
Poole C. H.	*The Customs, Superstitions and Legends of the County of Stafford*	1876
Prince N.H.	*Old West Bromwich*	1924
Price M.	*Folk Tales and Legends of Warwickshire*	1982
Raven J.	*The Folklore of Staffordshire*	1978
Ridland E. M.	*Ballads of old Birmingham and Neighbourhood*	1951
Travis P.	*In Search of the Supernatural*	1975
Vaughan J. E.	*The Parish Church and Ancient Grammar School of King's Norton*	1969
Vaughan T.	*Tales of Sutton Town and Chase*	1904

Westwood Press Publications

THE ROYAL TOWN of SUTTON COLDFIELD
A Commemorative History   by Douglas V. Jones
Running to 208 pages and covering the period from Saxon times up till 1974, when the Royal Town of Sutton Coldfield was amalgamated with Birmingham this is a warm human story of local people, events and landmarks.

SUTTON COLDFIELD 1974-1984 The Story of a Decade
The Modern sequel to the History of Sutton   by Douglas V. Jones
A lavishly illustrated Chronicle which recalls the many changes to the face of Sutton since its merger with Birmingham, together with a Pictorial Supplement, *Sutton in 1984.*

SUTTON PARK Its History and Wildlife   by Douglas V. Jones
Profusely illustrated with a wide selection of old and new pictures most of which have not previously been published, complete with centrefold map, and detailed with three interesting walks short enough for the casual walker to take at leisure.

STEAMING UP TO SUTTON How the Birmingham to Sutton
Coldfield Railway Line was built in 1862   written by Roger Lea
Every day thousands travel on the railway line between Sutton and Birmingham, without giving much thought to its origins and history. This is the fascinating story.

THE STORY OF ERDINGTON
From Sleepy Hamlet to Thriving Suburb   by Douglas V. Jones
Tracing the history of Erdington from earliest times, through the ages up to the late twentieth century. With some ninety-eight illustrations including a period map circa 1880.

MEMORIES OF A TWENTIES CHILD   by Douglas V. Jones
A nostalgic trip into one man's childhood and youth during the years between the wars. The book is a profusely illustrated reminder of the age of steam, gas-lamps, crystal-sets and tramcars.

DURATION MAN 1939-46   My War, by Douglas V. Jones
An enthralling sequel to "Memories of a Twenties Child"
This is the story of some of those who fought the good fight against red tape, boredom and gloom in places where all three were often present. If from time to time it may appear that soldiering is a mug's game, then the reader must draw his own conclusions. 144 pages, fully illustrated.

THE BOOK OF BRUM or Mekya Selfa Tum   by Ray Tennant
Random thoughts on the dialect and accent of the Second City (Brumslang) with a glossary of the most common expressions plus Brumodes, Brumverse and Brumericks with a little more serious verse. Brilliantly illustrated with appropriate cartoons by Jim Lyndon.

Last Tram Down The Village and Other Memories of
YESTERDAY'S BIRMINGHAM   by Ray Tennant
Although all the places written about are centred in or very near to Birmingham it will, hopefully, be of interest to people who live in other cities since many of the memories could be shared and appreciated by anyone who lived through the traumatic years of the thirties and forties.